What People Are Saying about ...g

This is a great book about working in teams because it is based on a deep understanding of people and strategy. This is not a book that every leader needs to display in pristine condition on her shelf. Instead it is a book that every leader should buy in bulk, hand out to colleagues, and will take delight in only when the majority of its pages become seriously coffee-stained.

Dr. Laurence S. Lyons,
series editor and author *Coaching for Leadership*,
creator of Dr. Fink stories, and visiting academic fellow at Henley Business School

Intelligent, insightful and interesting—*Top Teaming* is a "must-read" for every leader and corporate executive seeking to crack the code on how to raise the bar of the teams they manage and those they are a part of. Larry Levin is not just a compelling writer; he is a real practitioner of the art and science of developing great teams!

DSM, SVP, Fortune 100 Manufacturing

The cold hard reality of work life today is that so much of what we do depends upon the success of others. But getting people to work together—and like it—is no easy task. It is a challenge that all leaders face. For them—and for those who work in teams—*Top Teaming* by Dr. Larry Levin is a gift. Dr. Levin breaks down the nature of teamwork into what works and what does not. Well-written and full of insight, *Top Teaming* is a resource that individuals and organizations will find indispensable.

John Baldoni,
internationally recognized leadership coach, columnist,
and author of *Lead By Example and Lead Your Boss*.

This book brings to all the benefit of the talents already enjoyed by those who have worked with Dr. Larry Levin. *Top Teaming* does exactly what it says it will do: guides executives on how to create and maintain the super-performing teams needed to compete and win in this increasingly complex twenty-first century business world. Read it or lose.

Iain Melville, CEO, RCD

Health care isn't what it used to be, and will never again be what it is today. Navigating an industry where quality improvement is paramount, leadership needs to continually improve. *Top Teaming: A Road Map for Teams Navigating the Now, the New, and the Next* is an excellent source and inspiration for all health-care leaders in one of their most important activities—working together to achieve excellence.

Don Mueller, Executive Director,
Marcus Autism Center &V.P. Strategy and Business Development,
Children's Healthcare of Atlanta

Physicians are groomed to compete one against another as a sign of intellect; thus, the notion of teaming can be strongly resisted. In this new era of health-care reform, collaboration between providers and with hospital administrators will not be optional. Dr Levin knows the medical landscape and provides a user-friendly template to help team members maximize the function of already high-value teams. He has coached our group to a much higher performance.

Robert Campbell, MD,
Director, Sibley Heart Center

A new "high" has been attained with *Top Teaming*. Larry's fresh, insightful guidance goes well beyond the usual "high-performance teams" strategies. A seasoned practitioner's sharp eye on the realities of today's business environment translates into timely road maps that I will most definitely integrate into my teaming plans.

Lisa Fanto,
VP Human Resources,
Hardin Construction Group

For a global company, the importance of building executive teams that understand how to manage the "Now and the New" is perhaps the most important criteria in achieving both operational success and strategic advantage in a fast-changing world. *Top Teaming: A Road Map for Teams Navigating the Now, the New, and the Next* is an excellent source and inspiration for all leaders in one of their most important activities—working together.

MC, COO, Global Pharmaceutical Firm

TOP
TEAMING

A Roadmap for
Leadership Teams
Navigating the Now,
the New, and the Next

Dr. Lawrence S. Levin

Foreword by Marshall Goldsmith

iUniverse, Inc.
Bloomington

Top Teaming
A Roadmap for Leadership Teams Navigating
the Now, the New, and the Next

iUniverse books may be ordered through booksellers or by contacting:

iUniverse
1663 Liberty Drive
Bloomington, IN 47403
www.iuniverse.com
1-800-Authors (1-800-288-4677)

ISBN: 978-1-4620-3677-6 (sc)
ISBN: 978-1-4620-3678-3 (hc)
ISBN: 978-1-4620-3679-0 (e)

Library of Congress Control Number: 2011911457

Printed in the United States of America

iUniverse rev. date: 08/05/2011

Dedication

To my own *Top Team*—my family—whose deep emotional, relational, and collective intelligence is an ongoing source of wonderment to me: my wife and partner, Dr. Patricia Wheeler; my lovely and smart daughters, Amy and Stephanie; and my mom, Ruth, who, while she doesn't understand what I do for a living, is still proud of me.

Larry Levin 2011

TABLE OF CONTENTS

FOREWORD

A few years ago, Larry Levin and I stood in his driveway, and I asked him, "What do you want to be known for?" A powerful question, I've asked it of myself, my clients, and my friends over the years. It's served to both focus and inspire many of us to be successful at what we most want to do. Larry said he wanted to be known for helping leaders to build great teams—an admirable answer and one for which there is much work for him to do!

This is because the traditional, hierarchical school of leadership is giving way to a new focus on networked team leadership. Leaders are members of all different sorts of teams, from virtual to autonomous, from cross-functional to action-learning. However, the common challenge faced by today's leaders is the necessity of building teams in an environment of rapid change with limited resources.

And, this is where *Top Teaming: A Road Map for Leadership Teams Navigating the Now, the New, and the Next* fills a huge gap. *Top Teaming* is about the conversations that extraordinary leaders and their teams have and the practices that they do that differentiate them from good, "high-performance teams," and make them exceptional, high-caliber Top Teams. Simply put, it is about how good teams get even better to become great teams in an increasingly complex world.

It is written from the viewpoint of an experienced practitioner—someone who has been a trusted advisor to CEOs and executive leadership teams for twenty years across a wide range of industries and geographies. Larry understands how great leaders develop and thus develop their Top Teams. This is a very pragmatic and realistic book written by a guy who has seen it from the boardroom to the shop floor.

Whether you are a CEO, senior leader, team leader, or team member, reading *Top Teaming: A Road Map for Leadership Teams Navigating the Now, the New, and the Next* will help you take your team to the next level—the exceptional level of a Top Team!

Life is good!

Marshall Goldsmith
World-renowned executive educator and
author of the *New York Times* bestsellers
MOJO and *What Got You Here Won't Get You
There*

ACKNOWLEDGMENTS

This book would never have been written if not for the many clients that opened their doors and their professional lives to me. It was through being with these Top Teams during the toughest of times that forged the foundations of this book and the practices therein. It is a rare privilege to work with such committed, smart, and caring people. I am very thankful to them and thankful that I get to do this work for a living.

I also want to give special thanks to my editor, Sarah McArthur, who was a joy to work with and made the process fun. And to the irrepressible and always inspiring Marshall Goldsmith, who was perceptive enough to ask me what I wanted to be known for and courageous enough to challenge me to go do it.

Being in this business for twenty years has exposed me to a world of wonderful, dedicated, and unbelievably competent consultants, colleagues, and teachers. To all of you I humbly say, "Thank you."

Larry Levin 2011

INTRODUCTION

FOR THE PAST TWENTY YEARS, I have worked closely with executive teams within global Fortune 1000 and midcap companies across the span of health care, financial services, manufacturing, life sciences, and technology.

I have helped senior teams learn to navigate growth, manage significant and complex change, and address the new and ever-changing global marketplace and economies. These experienced teams have had to react to sudden shifts in political and economic conditions and commodity prices, as well as to global mergers and rapid, unexpected market changes. They have had to simultaneously think of how to courageously grow a business while "bottom-proofing" it against a downturn. These are smart people doing what is "business as usual" for a Top Team—or at least should be. And these teams are both committed and ultimately responsible for setting and executing strategy, for ensuring financial results, and for securing a future for their employees. *Top Teaming* is the culmination of the knowledge and experiences I have had with Top Teams—and those striving to be Top Teams—over these many years.

In all my experience, the sudden, intense, global economic shifts beginning in 2008 have had the most significant impact on how Top Teams and their leaders work together to navigate through both bad times and good. Virtually unprecedented, nearly every individual and company across the world has been impacted and influenced by the Great Recession. And, as the speed of change continues to accelerate, and as volatility, complexity, and ambiguity increase, the interconnectedness of the global marketplace becomes even more apparent. We saw irresponsible and unsustainable investment and banking practices in the United States impact stock markets in India, dropping commodity prices caused by reduced demand decimating growing economies in Russia and Ireland, and the European Union's struggles impacting global companies everywhere. I've watched in amazement at the enormous ripple effects that occurred when historically stable organizations teetered on the verge of insolvency during the recent economic crisis. Those that rebounded were deeply changed.

The effects of the crisis are not just centered on the financial and manufacturing sectors: major pharmaceutical organizations are under attack and must balance the complex equations of risk, benefit, profit, and politics. Significant changes and new legislation in the healthcare and health sciences industries have forced everyone from large hospital and academic medicine systems to physician practices and payor systems to redefine how they operate and think through the cultural, behavioral, structural, and leadership changes they need to survive. And the list goes on.

The interconnected world that we are just beginning to understand is suddenly very real and uncertain. Predictability and control, the two major variables in how we experience stress, are diminished. The world in which we live suddenly seems much more complex and ambiguous. This is what I mean when I talk about the "New Normal." Clearly, those of us who have been on the playing field for many years do not expect a return to an earlier time that seemed more predictable and less volatile. In fact, the amount of CEO and senior-level turnover has significantly increased, perhaps in parallel with the increasing complexity and ever-increasing challenges posed by a fast-changing world.

These are tough times for top executive teams, who are faced with a new series of challenges and paradoxes that require new mindsets and thinking about driving success. The questions they must ask themselves are many and difficult. For instance:

- How do we set a strategy when external forces and technologies shift so quickly?

- How do we bottom-proof our company and grow at the same time?

- How do we focus on innovation while ensuring we really pay attention to the "basics" of our business?

- How do we maximize collaboration and develop the people beneath us when we have virtually no time to do so?

- How can we think together as a team and align the organization behind our most critical priorities, which can and will shift and change in response to the changing world around us?

- How do we get the most out of our teams and our people?

Top Teams carry with them tremendous collective intelligence (CI) in their deep operating experience, and have the ability to exert significant influence over their company's direction, mindset, focus, and performance. They have both the opportunity and obligation to navigate big change and make a significant difference in the future of their organizations. Ultimately, they are responsible for dealing with both the "Now and the New"—the current realities and the evolving future.

While all Top Teams have this responsibility, only some do it well. Even fewer do it well when under tremendous stress and pressure. In my research and interviews with senior leaders, I have found that there are ten essential groups of practices that differentiate Top Teams from groups of talented and hardworking individuals. These are the "must-do's" that make the difference between great teams that drive great results and everybody else.

This book is about the practices that create and sustain Top Teams. It is a "how-to" book about raising the bar of evolving and experienced senior teams' abilities to think and execute together over time and create the results they have promised to their stockholders, stakeholders, and employees. It is about how to drive responsibility and alignment down the organization so they grow teams at all levels that are capable, accountable, and engaged. It is about how those in leadership positions exercise the self-knowledge and deliberateness to create a legacy of success that is sustainable over time. It is designed to serve as a road map to help struggling teams become good teams and already good teams to become even better.

This book is divided into ten chapters that represent the ten essential practices of Top Teams.

- Chapter 1 focuses on establishing the foundation of a Top Team, clarifying what the team is truly *for* and establishing the power of a collective and agreed-upon future.

- Chapter 2 explores the critical elements in defining and building a Top Team. This chapter looks at the essential elements of managing critical intersections within and across the organization, and addressing the issues that matter most in setting the culture and calibrating desired behaviors within the team.

- Chapter 3 addresses the current demands on leaders within complex organizations—how to deal simultaneously with the Now and the New, how to understand and manage paradox, and how to focus on creating excellence in execution while exploring an innovative future.

- Chapter 4 asks the question "has the nature of change somehow changed?" It suggests that there are different models of change and that leadership teams must both welcome change and actively lead through periods of complex change.

- Chapter 5 is about how Top Teams must navigate complexity, make critical decisions, and fully engage their organizations in managing the Now, the New, and the Next.

- Chapter 6 focuses on the Art of the Advance: How good teams get even better through the power of deliberately focused dialogue.

- Chapter 7 explores what it takes to grow and sustain a Top Team. It raises the importance of relational intelligence (RI) as a critical factor in increasing trust within a team and throughout an organization.

- Chapter 8 represents a strong point of view about how great teams require great leaders and what is required to grow, coach, and develop both experienced and emerging leaders.

- Chapter 9 focuses on integrating the power of a team through deliberately increasing and using its collective intelligence (CI).

- Chapter 10 challenges already high-performing teams to raise the bar and become a Top Team that has both the ability and willingness to drive growth, execute with excellence, and promote a legacy of success.

One of my favorite quotes is that "the measure of a person's intelligence is not measured by what he knows, but by the quality of the questions he asks." Great leaders and Top Teams continually ask the right questions. As you read the book I encourage you to use the questions at the end of each chapter and in the appendix to examine and raise your game. Think about your team, those teams that report to you, and those teams that you report to, and ask the question, "How can we get even better?" In this way, you will begin to practice the words of management visionary Peter Drucker, who said, "The leader of the past knew how to tell; the leader of the future knows how to ask."

CHAPTER 1

Setting the Cornerstone: Being Truly FOR Something

DAVID WAS NAMED GENERAL MANAGER *of a highly profitable division of a large manufacturing firm. A very ambitious and forward-thinking leader, he wanted to reshape the historic command-and-control culture and build a leadership team that could use its collective intellect and experience to grow the organization by reshaping its business model and leadership approach. He inherited a culture that was, by most external standards, quite successful and profitable— never having missed a promise to the company or to stockholders. The team was smart, hardworking, and proud of their operational excellence. David's questions for himself and his team were: "How can this team get even better? How can we grow in global reach, innovation, and profitability? How can we begin to think more strategically and more globally?" And, "How can we 'raise the bar' of our performance?"*

1

Working with David, our firm decided to schedule an "Advance" (not a Retreat) for his team of direct reports. (Read more about how to plan Advances in chapter 6.) We began this process by interviewing each team member and performing a thorough diagnosis to measure how well the team thought it was doing. We began the actual Advance by presenting data from the interviews to the assembled group. People were surprised at the level of agreement and the passion within the team around their real desire to be more strategic, to think together more deeply, and to take the team to a new level. They knew that it would not be easy and that it would require changes in their dynamics and their willingness to surface and resolve real issues. They understood that it would challenge the very culture that had given them a track record of success.

This Advance was the start of a journey that would, over the next eighteen months, dramatically change the nature, dynamics, accountability, ownership, performance, and even the definition of the team as its members moved from operating as a great collection of individual performers to operating as a Top Team.

Being Truly for Something: The Power of a Collective Future

There is always a beginning. Even for experienced teams that have worked together for years, there are those times when the team must step back and re-ask the fundamental and significant questions about their direction—where they are headed. This is not an uncommon practice on the surface, as virtually every team and organization has a "vision" and strategic plan. What is uncommon, however, and what represents the first critical waypoint in a Top Team's journey, is the articulation of a uniting common purpose and a clear and agreed vision of a desired future—in other words, what the team is truly *for*.

This is the key aligning principle of a Top Team and the start of its journey as it begins to define the intersection of leadership direction, organizational concern, and current reality. To be sure, this is a very different process from writing a typical vision or mission statement, which often becomes more of a slogan than a deep source of gravity, focus, and commitment. To go through a process of defining what a Top Team is *for* requires honest, deep, and ongoing dialogue among the members of a senior team and throughout the organization about current realities, real possibilities, and what must and must not change in order to secure the future of the organization.

Everything must be on the table as teams redefine success and survival. As Mickey Connolly writes, "The source of teamwork is a common future" (Connolly and Rionoshek 2002, 145).

So we began the Advance with David's team by asking them what they were really *for*. This sounds like a simple question, yet the dialogue lasted four hours. We revisited strategy. We talked about what had changed, what was changing, and their ability to control their own destinies. We looked at the business while wearing an "enterprise hat." And they asked themselves whether they should, or even could, raise the bar of their performance as an executive team.

In the course of the dialogue, something broke open—and the team began to define what the future could and should look like. Again, this was happening within a

> What represents the first critical waypoint in a Top Team's journey is the articulation of a uniting common purpose and a clear and agreed vision of a desired future—in other words, what the team is truly for.

company that prided itself on hitting its numbers and operating with the reliability and operational excellence that would make a Six-Sigma black belt proud. This was a different dialogue that redefined the future. It was not an "either/or" but a "both/and" dialogue that spoke to how the company could dramatically make the changes that would allow it to realize a competitive difference and a different future. This would allow it to not only survive but also to prevail in the marketplace while not missing a beat in its core business.

As David described after the initial session:

"We realized that we had to do more than just make our numbers and build the best product every moment of every day. We became very clear that we were a "growth engine" of this firm, that we are *for* 30 percent growth, integrating all our global businesses and collaborating across geographies, developing the next generation(s) of leaders, and continuing to drive operational excellence and safety within all our plants. We are *for* building this team and those that report to us and creating the culture, behaviors, and individual commitment to significantly change our approach to our business."

When Vision and Reality Collide

There is an old saying (von Goethe, Wolfgang, date unknown) that *"love is an ideal thing, marriage a real thing; a confusion of the ideal and the real never goes unpunished."* And so it is with the collision between vision and reality. Vision is an idealized state—something to which companies aspire. Vision is formed when the senior team goes on an off-site and envisions the desired future of the firm. It is, by definition and by its very nature, a state that organizations rarely reach. And, cynically, it is that poster in the lunchroom that most people see but don't see.

About four years ago, I was at the corporate headquarters of a fast-growing pharmaceutical company having lunch with a group of managers. The food was terrific, the view of the lake and Japanese maples was exquisite, and the vision statement on the wall-mounted plasma monitors was inspiring as it scrolled over the waterfall backdrop. I commented as to what an inspiring vision it was. One of the managers briefly paused in midbite as he said tersely, "It's a lie." I was struck by his candor and his bitterness and realized at that moment that no false promise, no matter how aspirational or inspirational, ever goes unpunished. The gap between what was written and what was real, between what was said and what was done, between talk and walk, was significant—and it greatly impacted the workforce. Turnover, just after bonus time, was significant. Major initiatives were delayed and postponed as they were constantly getting new people up to speed. Competitors entering the market quickly gobbled up talented ex-employees. And management team members seemed to have no clue. In their case, the "light at the end of the tunnel" (as represented by their vision) was indeed the headlight of an approaching train. They had a vision but could not define what they were *for* in ways that key people understood and could support. And because of this, they could not craft a going-forward strategy that made sense and that people could align behind.

Ensuring that you have a vision that is not at odds with reality is essential to the intellectual and psychological makeup of a workforce. And it is the full and complete responsibility of the senior team, which must utilize the vision as a "stretch" to connect current realities to a desired future. As my partner, Dr. Patricia Wheeler (personal communication), reminds me, "It's not what a vision is, it's what it does." A workforce is always watching the leaders' feet to see if they are walking the talk. And this is even truer in times of increased turbulence and complexity.

As executive teams think about and work toward aligning their organizations, defining clear priorities, setting goals, and consciously instilling a culture that can perform, they have to ensure that they have a terrific grasp on current realities, which include external influences, political and global circumstances, changes in technologies, customer issues, and their own capabilities. They also have to be aware of their internal realities, which include history, culture, behaviors, and competencies. As we will see, defining the composition and competencies of teams and growing experienced and evolving teams into even better functioning Top Teams requires defining a vision going forward and having a strong grasp of current and emerging reality.

Strategy as Purpose

I have yet to meet a leader who has not experienced off-sites or retreats in which strategy was discussed, good ideas surfaced, and promises were made. In fact, I rarely ask CEOs about their strategic plans without them turning in their seats and hauling out a large binder or two ("credenza ware") containing a very thorough, smart, and expensive strategic plan. Yet when I ask them how the execution of the plan is proceeding, I usually hear their disappointment in their lack of progress and often hear some excellent explanations having to do with managing crises that unexpectedly showed up, not having the time to take on new things, or waiting for a new and key person to join the team. Everything they say is true. Yet the fact is that the senior team has not advanced the ball as promised. In addition, the organization has just spent a boatload of money on smart consultants to build a strategic map for them, even though the accuracy of long-term strategic planning is more in question than ever and "directional correctness" with frequent course corrections is more the norm.

It is quite possible to stay true to a long-term vision while knowing that the path to achieve it has been radically changed. It is also possible that the very identity and vision of a company must be dramatically shifted, forcing leaders to change direction in ways that were never predicted. This is not all that unusual in times when mergers between competitors, once thought unimaginable, have become an everyday occurrence.

Brian Kesseler of Johnson Controls (personal conversation) describes asking his team to "challenge everything you've ever thought," as decisions that made sense six months ago may not apply today. As a CEO of a large defense firm said to me, "We are having conversations we would never have had a year ago. We're forced to look at things differently. We're forced to anticipate what we might do today that will be absolutely wrong for the future." As these executives expressed, leaders need to drive this conversation and be open to it. And they need to remember that nobody solves problems of this complexity on their own.

Dynamically, this is where teams demonstrate courage, as they must both take on and manage risk while, at the same time, look for opportunities to grow. And this must occur in an environment of openness, collaboration, and engagement as the world continues to churn and change. Defining this future, taking strategy into execution, is the senior purpose of leadership teams. The process

> "We are having conversations we would never have had a year ago. We're forced to look at things differently. We're forced to anticipate what we might do today that will be absolutely wrong for the future."

of truly defining the future is essential to aligning both leadership teams at all levels and the entirety of the employee body.

This process requires real and ongoing dialogue among the senior team and throughout the organization about current realities and what must and must not change in order to secure their future. Everything must be on the table as teams redefine success and survival. As a senior leader in a large pharmaceutical company told us, "We have to get past how we have historically looked at things; overcome our classic objections, such as, 'We've never done it that way' or 'That won't work here'; and move the conversation forward."

This is strategy that is not static, but is dynamic and purposeful. It is fueled by a Top Team that is willing to put everything on the table. It drives organizational agility, which, as we have seen in the economic meltdown of 2008–2009, represents the difference between survival and catastrophe.

Individual and Collective Commitment

We've talked about the need to articulate the senior purpose of a team—what the team is truly *for*. At both the individual and collective levels, it is about defining the one or two collective and "audacious" goals that far exceed the individual goals of individual leaders. Yet, we have also seen that it is not unusual for teams to struggle to stay on track and keep their eyes on the larger prize.

What we are talking about here is changing the nature of the dialogue that occurs within most senior teams, thus changing the very dynamics of the team. As David, in the example we used earlier, said, "If we think we are doing things well, we are probably shooting only layups." This is an easy sports analogy, to be sure, but if you think about how the nature of the game and the level of competition are changing, it is highly appropriate. The game is more complex than ever and, as the senior VP of a global beverage firm said to his team recently, "We are all facing the same problems. It is about who gets there first wins."

Individual and collective responsibility is essential in executing any forward-looking strategy. Leaders have to "sign up for the experiences that are valued." They must understand and manage the paradox of achieving both individual and collective goals, and unleash the urgency and passion throughout the organization about what they are *for*. This is essential, but it is not easy.

There is little doubt that time is the great commodity for members of senior teams. They are usually so deeply involved in the running of their businesses or functions that they cannot take on much more. Their incentive compensation, which is often tied to the achievement of their individual and group goals, understandably drives where they place their focus. One obvious solution for them is to grow the capabilities of their teams of direct reports to better handle the day-to-day operational engine. By delegating decisions down to the next level, senior leaders have more bandwidth to architect and drive key strategies. The paradox is that most senior leaders don't have the time to develop their key people to this stage, and they cannot afford for key balls to be dropped during a learning curve. This is an obvious problem on the surface, which is only corrected by taking greater individual and collective (team) responsibility to grow and develop identified high potentials and teams of direct reports. How does a senior team, in which time is a key commodity and individual achievement is rewarded (and failure noticed), address this paradox?

> "If we think we are doing things well, we are probably shooting only layups."

David's team, for example, made their Strategic Talent

Review exercise an energetic and challenging process by linking the senior team members' bonuses to the accomplishment of the key developmental goals for *all* their high potentials. Think about that—collective and individual responsibility in growing *each* key person one level down. No doubt this impacted the discussion and group dynamics within the senior team. It set off debate, drove collaboration, and pushed people to operate across boundaries, *and* it allowed the senior team to move closer to reality and what it was ultimately *for*.

This is but one example of demonstrating individual and group commitment, but the back story here centers on the tough dialogue that must occur within a team about how to make these goals real. To quote Ram Charan (2001), "Dialogue is the essential unit of work." And this is not automatic, or particularly easy, in most teams.

Questions

Being Truly *FOR* Something:
The Power of a Collective Future

- To what extent is your senior purpose—what you are *for*—clearly understood?

- How well has this been articulated? Does it have passion?

- Can you state it convincingly?

- Does the organization know it? Do individuals know what this means for them and what is expected of them?

When Vision and Reality Collide

- How well is the vision of your company understood? Does it represent a desired future for the firm?

- How well do you have your hands around the external realities of your business? What about your internal realities, capabilities, and limitations?

- Is there a credibility gap between what the senior team has said and what it has done? Are the current realities well articulated and understood by the workforce?

Strategy as Purpose

- How "actionable" is your strategic plan? What must the team do to make it even better?

- Are all members clear on how their role drives the plan?

- What is the quality of dialogue within your team? What needs to occur to make it even more open and candid?

Individual and Collective Commitment

- To what extent are you held individually accountable for the success of the team?

- To what extent does the team hold itself collectively accountable?

- What would happen if you raised the bar of collective accountability?

CHAPTER 2

Aligning the Stars

SEVERAL YEARS AGO, THE LEVIN Group was asked to consult in a health-care system where two powerful, successful, and sizable medical practices were considering a merger. The attorneys and accountants had created a compelling business case. A health-care consulting firm had created a suggested management structure based on a well-thought-out strategic plan that would provide growth, increased profitability, and a more efficient distribution of effort. Yet on two occasions, at the eleventh hour, negotiations broke down. Clearly this was not caused by a lack of due diligence. Nor was it simply a case of cold feet. What was occurring was the emergence of historic mistrust fueled by twenty years of competition between the senior players. Dialogue had broken down, and thus so did the deal.

Building a new leadership team that could align the organizations in the service of the larger purpose, take on the tough issues that were predictable but difficult, address issues of turf and control, and build a senior *team that was collaborative, direct, dynamic, and successful seemed a very difficult task. This team worked over a period of nearly three years on "aligning the stars"—consciously and deliberately building a Top Team that could and did take on the challenges before it and create a top-notch health-care system.*

Once you have clearly defined the senior purpose of your team—what your team is *for*—you can then begin the process of designing and aligning your team behind it. While the need for alignment seems obvious on the surface, it is a critical and often difficult process.

Questions that must be asked are:

- Given the mission and purpose of the organization, what kind of team do we need to be to accomplish it?
- Do we have the right people on the bus?
- How should we be structured to optimize decisions?
- What are our critical priorities and accountabilities?
- Where are our critical interdependencies?
- How do we best reach across functions and geographies?
- How do we work together to lead the organization in these times?
- What does it mean to be a leader in this company today?

These questions, and others that follow, may sound simple, but there are no easy answers. This is iterative dialogue, as there is no one right way to design a team. Thus it is very important that leadership teams sustain a dialogue around alignment and take the time to move issues from implicit and not well understood, to fully explicit, expressed, and defined agreements.

Since the corporate environment today is not business as usual, Top Teams must continually reexamine how they work together in the service of the mission. In other words, they must constantly redefine themselves as a team. Two seemingly opposed default settings are at work: On the one hand, the senior team has a common objective—survival in the face of external threat—that tends to pull people together. On the other hand, environments of uncertainty and scarcity drive more "tribal" behaviors: people hold on tight to their jobs, functions, teams, or information in an attempt to maximize security. The antidote to these almost automatic and autonomic responses is to create a conscious and deliberate environment at the top that is dedicated and continues to examine how its members are working together in the service of the mission. This is a classic case of "the Soft Stuff Driving the Hard Stuff."

One Size Does Not Fit All: What Kind of Team Do We Need to Be?

Once a team has begun the process of articulating its senior purpose, it needs to define what kind of team it must be to accomplish it. There is no textbook answer. Simply put, the type of team that is needed and how members must operate together depend completely on what this team needs to do in the service of the organization's strategic and critical priorities.

When we work with teams, we often begin by drawing a horizontal line on a board. This represents a continuum of interdependency. On the far left is a team that requires low interdependency, such as a bowling team, whose members each add up their best individual scores. On the far right is a highly interdependent team, such as a Navy SEAL team, whose very lives depend on one another. Somewhere in the middle are typically examples of sports teams—football and basketball, in which the roles must be clear, interdependency is essential, and winning or losing happens together. We begin by asking the team where it currently falls within the continuum and, given what it has said about its desired future, where the level of interdependency needs to be. (See Figure 2.1.)

(Figure 2.1) Interdependency

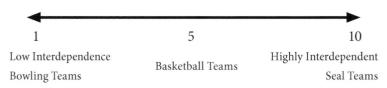

1	5	10
Low Interdependence	Basketball Teams	Highly Interdependent
Bowling Teams		Seal Teams

Questions
On a scale of 1-10, with 10 representing high interdependence
    1) Where do you see your team now?
    2) How interdependent does your team need to be?
    3) What must you do to close this gap?

What we find is always interesting and informative. Most intact teams that are comprised of experienced people with operational and functional backgrounds express a clear need for higher interdependency as they set and begin to move toward more ambitious and higher-level goals. They know, as Marshall Goldsmith (2007) would say, "what got them here won't get them there." And there are organizations that are specific about exactly where they must be more collaborative as a team and where they can continue to operate as they are. Portfolio companies, for example, in which business lines are separate and independent, can operate as successful and appropriate "bowling teams." Yet even in cases of low interdependence, we find areas in which greater connectedness and collaboration, often driven from the functional areas, help these teams optimize. There are usually areas, sometimes subtle,

"There is no one 'right' type of team or structure. It completely depends on what a team is tasked to do—again, what it is *for.*"

sometimes surprising, where the team members find greater synergy and find ways to reduce costs and redundancy, and to utilize one another's expertise to drive even better results. Simply put, there is no one "right" type of team or structure. It completely depends on what a team is tasked to do—again, what it is *for*.

As a team, once we begin to define the type of team we need to be in order to accomplish the senior purpose, there are some difficult conversations that must occur. Often these occur between the CEO and his or her trusted advisors, and sometimes they occur in the room within the team. The question of whether the team has the "right people on the bus," as Jim Collins (2001) in *Good to Great* states, is a difficult yet essential question. In our work as executive coaches, we are often called upon to help assess and develop executives who have to grow in their roles and capabilities to contribute to a Top Team. It is a demand and a stretch to play at this level.

Many executives can, in fact, grow in their roles and do so enthusiastically. Yet for some, this new demand is seen as a breaking of a social contract and not what they signed up for. How the composition of the new team is decided and how changes are made in roles and structure are critical processes involving building trust, clarifying expectations, managing anxiety, and beginning the process of communicating change to the larger employee body. It is a necessary but tough thing to do.

Defining and Managing the Critical Intersections

As teams come together and begin to have the forward-thinking dialogue about how they need to operate, several critical conversations begin to occur. The first is deciding how to best structure around the expressed level of interdependency. The typical vertical corporate structure of business units with support functions and teams of direct reports is usually cumbersome and slow. Matrix organizations are designed to maximize flow of products or services by minimizing the numbers of redundant functions within each division or unit and by increasing collaboration between operational and functional areas. Yet matrix organizations are often seen as unwieldy and hard to navigate.

This is where the process of identifying and managing critical intersections occurs. Simply put, the easiest and most elegant way to navigate a matrix is to map the organization, identify those people with whom you have to have successful outcomes, then go out and, as Brian Kesseler (personal conversation) of Johnson Control says, "Make and cut your deals." What Brian means here is that people who are involved in any critical intersection, whether it involves working across a matrix, in an intersection between a functional and an operational area, or who operate as teams of people that pursue similar customers, must connect with one another, define what is important to them, listen for what is important to others, affirm what is important to the organization, and then make (and keep) agreements. This is relational intelligence (RI) at its finest, which accomplishes several things concurrently: It builds those critical relationships within the informal organization; it accelerates decision-making and accountability as the right people are talking directly to one another about what matters; and it makes a complex structure significantly easier to navigate in the service of the customer. It also serves to free up senior leaders, who are not asked nearly as often to make day-to-day decisions and can thus spend more time on the larger issues critical for the senior team. A CFO of a major financial institution commented that the "ticket of admission" for her to think strategically was how well the people who reported to her were handling operational issues across the global organization. She was surprised at how few ties she had to break and how few impasses made it to her desk.

Identifying and managing those critical intersections is an important step in creating collaboration and minimizing turf or tribe. It also drives employee engagement as employees one to three levels below the Top Team make decisions that support critical priorities, grow in their roles and capabilities, and deliver faster responses to customer needs.

Trust over Peace:
Addressing and Resolving the Issues that Matter

One of the most essential yet difficult variables that distinguishes Top Teams from most executive teams is their ability to engage in honest, candid, and authentic dialogue. Dialogue (from the Greek *dia-logos*) literally means an exchange of ideas. In our work with teams, and in our observation of Top Teams, there is a high premium put on addressing the most important and often the most difficult issues within the team setting, with an eye toward resolving them. Jake Jackson, retired executive of a large financial institution, talks about how teams can choose to prioritize peace over trust or vice versa. (Jackson personal conversation) Most of us have experienced this when we have participated in polite, careful, and indirect teams. In this dynamic, issues may be noted, but they are not explored in depth. At worst, civility in public gives rise to passive-aggressive or indirect behavior in private as members of teams talk over the water cooler or an adult beverage about those very issues that should be on the table.

In Top Teams, the opposite must occur—trust must be even more important than keeping the peace. This requires leaders to encourage, demand, and ensure that it is safe to talk openly about anything. As Sidney Taurel of Eli Lilly was widely attributed to say when opening the dialogue up for honest interactions, "Put the moose on the table." This is far easier said than done, as the culture of many firms is deeply "nice," yet indirect. Periodically, we hear the horror story of the executive who was shunned, banned, or fired for being too honest. In truth, this is rare. However, political correctness, carefulness, and less-than-direct conversation are often group behaviors and dynamics that we, as experienced consultants to this process, confront and work very hard to shift. As a Top Team builds, our role as advisors and consultants to this process is, in part, to know what is going on within both the formal and the informal organization. We utilize an ongoing interview process as an outside partner to the team that allows us to stay "tapped in" and thus know, and be able to surface, those issues that must be addressed and resolved by the senior team, and do so in an atmosphere that is mostly safe and risk-free.

There is an old line from theater that says, "Easier to act your way into feeling than feel your way into acting." For the dynamics of a team, this means that members begin, sometimes nervously, to address issues in depth and directly with one another with the clear intent of making their organization even better. The good news is that difficult dialogue becomes easier over time. Think of an issue that you talk about privately but not with your team. Think of a conversation that you've had with yourself in the car in which you said, "I wish I'd ..." or "I wish someone had ...." Think of a time when someone brought up an issue that mattered—that

> Great teams have a looseness about them—a deep and implicit trust that they are in this together.

everyone knew about but had never discussed. Those are the issues that are the grist for team dialogue. Great teams have a looseness about them—a deep and implicit trust that they are in this together. They have built a track record that allows them to talk through the tough issues.

Trust is a word that often arises as we explore the changing dynamics within a team. It has many meanings and underpinnings, but it is always a supercharged word. Driving operational excellence, representing someone's interests when they are not in the room, or simply being credible by making and keeping agreements are all part of building trust. Trust is far more important than peace when it comes to the crucible that is a Top Team. Great teams will tell you virtually every time that they now talk comfortably about issues that would never have surfaced in the past. Dave Myers (personal conversation), an SVP of Johnson Controls, talks about the necessity to "institutionalize conflict" among his team. Patrick Lencioni, in his very popular books the *The Five Dysfunctions of a Team* (Lencioni 2002) and *Death by Meeting* (Lencioni 2004), describes the importance of "mining for conflict" as a way of keeping teams honest and building trust. A good friend of ours known for his great Texas metaphors says about his team, "I'd rather have dogs you have to pull out of a fight than those you have to throw in." Trust over peace—the ability to have authentic and full dialogue about the issues that matter—is a critical and essential part of building Top Teams.

Shaving the Tiger: Understanding and Recalibrating the Default Setting of a Team

Part of understanding the collective self-knowledge that comprises the emotional intelligence (EI) of a team is to understand its default setting—what it is likely to do when under stress or operating on automatic pilot. Teams that have a history of operational focus go directly to the numbers and root-cause discussions when pressured. Health-care teams almost immediately argue about outcomes and support these arguments with data (then often argue about whose data is better). This default setting is not unlike our individual default settings when under stress. Do I move toward or away from others when pressured? What happens to my ability to trust? How do I cover my derriere when under threat? We know from the studies on EI that self-awareness is the first key step in recognizing our own default settings. It is equally true, though sometimes more difficult to recognize, what a team's default setting is when under the gun.

I was amazed (but somehow not surprised) to see, while watching a recent *Animal Planet* program, that when tigers are shaved, their stripes are also present in their skin. This says something about our fundamental personality or wiring, as the "who we are" goes deep—down to our very skins. Thus it is important to know (from an EI standpoint) who we are and what our default settings are likely to be individually and collectively. This is where people receive great value from leadership style instruments such as the Myers-Briggs, Hogan Suite, CDR 3-D Suite, DISC®, etc.

We work very deliberately to make these default settings both predictable and normal, often to the point of having teams rehearse and exaggerate pressure situations so they are less likely to go on autopilot. The antidote to moving away from real teaming when under threat is to adopt a conscious and deliberate style that says, "We know our default settings. If we find ourselves doing X (our default setting), someone will 'throw the flag' and revisit our agreements about how we will operate together." This collective team knowledge is like a fire alarm that gets the attention of the team members and returns them to the agreements they made about working together and resolving issues using the collective intelligence (CI) and support of the team.

Getting from "Yes" to "Hell Yes!"

We are often asked how to measure the progress of a team—what distinguishes good management and leadership teams from Top Teams. There are clearly external markers—how teams perform against their targets, engagement scores that measure the organization's sense of participation and involvement in the larger mission, self-assessment instruments in which teams rate themselves across a number of dimensions, and many more tangible and objective measures. There are also some dynamic, motivating, and powerful measures that drive Top Teams and give them the confidence, enthusiasm, and courage to take on the most challenging priorities and drive growth in the face of tough obstacles. These are internal and often subjective measures, yet they affirm the very real sense that the team is together and has the confidence, history, and collective horsepower to achieve virtually anything—together. This experience is described as "synergy," as "teamwork," and as operating with a "passionate focus" within the organization. In my observation, a team is always having fun as it moves from, "Well, this seems like a good idea," to "Hell yes! Let's do it!" This is aligning the stars at its finest.

Questions

ONE SIZE DOES NOT FIT ALL:
WHAT KIND OF TEAM DO WE NEED TO BE?

- Given the mission and purpose of the organization (what we are *for*), what kind of team do we need to be to accomplish these?

- What are our critical priorities and accountabilities?

- Do we have the right people on the bus?

- How should we be structured to optimize decisions?

- Where are our critical interdependencies? How do we best reach across functions and geographies?

- How do we work together to lead the organization in these times?

- What does it mean to be a leader in this company today?

DEFINING AND MANAGING THE CRITICAL INTERSECTIONS

- How do I best navigate the matrix and work across the enterprise?

- Have I created a system map that defines my critical intersections?

- Have I "made and cut my deals" with the people with whom I have critical interdependencies?

- Am I able, and willing, to be direct and honest with these people to ensure that all issues are on the table?

TRUST OVER PEACE:
ADDRESSING AND RESOLVING THE ISSUES THAT MATTER

- How direct am I (are we) with one another?

- To what extent do indirect, third-party conversations occur?

- How well have we "institutionalized conflict"? How willing are we to surface tough issues and talk them through?

- What issues, historical or current, get in the way of our ability to trust one another?

- Who do I have to build a better relationship with? When and how?

Shaving the Tiger: Understanding and Recalibrating the Default Setting of a Team

- How would I describe the "default setting" of our team when under pressure?

- What assessments or instruments have we used that have provided information on our individual and collective default settings?

- How well have we articulated the "rules of the road" and what to do to sustain real teamwork?

- How would I describe my personal default setting when under stress?

- How have we built a collective EI?

- How well do we know ourselves?

Getting from "Yes" to "Hell Yes!"

- How do you measure the progress of your team?

- What objective markers do you utilize to define progress?

- What are the subjective experiences that allow you to know, with a high degree of certainty, that you are moving forward as a team?

- What is your level of enthusiasm and optimism in moving forward with your team?

CHAPTER 3

Focusing on the Now and the New

Patricia is the senior vice president of operations at a large telecommunications organization, which has become successful by being dependable, predictable, and focusing on incremental improvement. She says with great pride that the organization has never missed a goal or a promise to the board. Yet, given the changes in the industry and the world, the organization is now seen as slow to respond to the market, and as not particularly innovative. So while the leadership team has created an ambitious growth plan, the organization as a whole is paradoxically hampered by those very things that have made it successful in the past.

Patricia was tasked with heading the team charged with driving innovation and creating a new business model at a time when the company was struggling to reduce costs, to confront new global competitors in the marketplace, and to satisfy old customers desirous of new technologies. At the same time, she had to ensure that sales and operations made their stated goals and that the nonnegotiables within her business, such as quality and safety, did not slip. As if that wasn't enough, she was working within a highly matrixed and geographically dispersed structure, which was, as is common in most businesses today, "leaned out." In other words, the organization had even fewer people to do even more. To top it off, Patricia headed up a leadership team that didn't yet have the skills and behaviors to operate in a horizontal and complex world. She described her day as, "trying to stand up and sit down at the same time." What Patricia experienced was the very real issue of having to deal with "the Now and the New."

The Now and the New

One of the greatest challenges for a senior team is how to manage the paradox of creating great visionary strategy that is innovative and future-focused while, at the same time, dealing with what we call "the fierce urgency of Now."

Most leadership teams are whipsawed by the seeming shifting demands and priorities of their board or marketplace. Some talk about having "corporate attention deficit" as they move from one set of priorities to another. To their credit, this is not abnormal, nor is it a judgment on their capability. It is a paradox, one of many that Top Teams must be able to understand, articulate, and address. Dealing with the Now and the New—at the same time—is the New Normal and

> "Dealing with the Now and the New—at the same time—is the New Normal and must be viewed as business as usual and a paradox to be managed."

must be viewed as business as usual and a paradox to be managed.

I recently asked a CEO how he was handling the new environment. He replied that if he couldn't find the real value in people and processes in these tough times, then he had no right to be leading the company—and that held true for his team as well. He went on to say that while they had to focus on the "real work," they also had to be scanning the environment for opportunities and growth. His point was that as markets adjust, discontinuities appear. Some competitors don't do well; thus, disruption creates opportunities. His responsibility was to keep the executive team focused on the present and the future at the same time—the Now and the New. Not an easy thing to do.

Encouraging and Normalizing Paradox

A critical skill set is a team's ability to understand and manage paradox—which means dealing with seemingly opposing forces when there is no clearly apparent right versus wrong. For instance, should the team focus on strategic growth or do they try to bottom-proof the company? Do they focus on the core business or look for new ways of operating? There is no one right answer. Identifying critical areas of paradox and managing them as a "both/and" versus a classic "either/or" decision is an essential navigational skill for a Top Team.

The concept of paradox in business was developed by Barry Johnson in his book *Polarity Management* (Johnson 1992, 1996). One of the core indicators of a paradox is when a team is faced with a decision or dilemma that does not have one long-term solution. It requires keeping two or more opposing or contradictory forces in balance. Thus, it is very different from a problem, which has, by definition, a solution. Think about it. Leadership teams are hardwired and highly incentivized to solve problems and make decisions. Yet, in real life, many if not most, of the big issues they discuss can't be solved by factual or analytic conversation alone. For instance, teams ask themselves: "How do we do more with fewer resources? How do we balance the global and local demands that we face? As we look to drive our culture forward, do we organize centrally or do we decentralize?" And on a more personal level: "How do we develop others but stay in control of our business? How do we both delegate and know the details?" And leaders ask themselves: "How do I maximize my division's performance and also be a team player? What are some of the key or confusing paradoxes I am facing?"

In our view, Top Teams have tremendous expertise, experience, and CI to address the most complex issues. Simply put, if they didn't have this capability, they wouldn't be considered a Top Team for long. Yet it is in harnessing the dialogue and intellectual rigor to balance the complex paradoxes that they face on a regular basis that Top Teams shine. We have a bias for dialogue within Top Teams about the most essential and difficult issues. We absolutely believe that Top Teams must be able to put the complex issues they face on the table and talk about them. This creates a paradox all on its own: when does a busy senior team find the time to deal with the big issues?

In our experience, this is where a regularly scheduled Advance is of critical importance. Ensuring that the agenda is "loose" enough creates the time for team members to get into the big, often ambiguous and complex issues they face. Highly agendized meetings are tough places within which to talk about complexity. Say, for example, the team has 10:00 a.m. to 10:45 a.m. scheduled on the agenda to discuss a big issue, such as whether to centralize a function or keep it more decentralized. Several things occur: They spend part of that time defining the issue to ensure they understand why it is on the table for them now. Different people weigh in—often with opinions of what should be done. Alternatives appear. There is the back and forth as team members provide history, experience, data, and so on to make their case. During this time, not everyone speaks. At ten thirty, someone says, "Look we only have fifteen minutes to resolve this." So what happens? Does the team vote, pass on the issue, table it, or assign it to a committee? Or does the leader thank people for their input with the intention of making the call later?

What Top Teams do well is to identify the critical issues (both strategic and tactical) that must be addressed and resolved. If they are, one, of essential importance, and, two, have the qualities of a paradox, then they label them as such and provide the two or three hours (or more) necessary to flesh out the issues. Again, a paradox is defined as such because it has no clear solutions. It is usually a dynamic balance of forces that leads the team members to ask, "How do we do this *and* that at the same time? How do we decide on a course of action while managing the opposing forces? How will we know when we need to rethink or rebalance? What indicators or alarms will tell us that we must revisit this issue?" These and many other questions are classic paradoxes—and it is essential that Top Teams have the awareness and the skill sets to understand, openly address, and manage them.

Driving the Fierce Urgency of "Now": The Need for Execution Excellence

One of our long-standing clients is a large food and beverage organization that has been rapidly expanding in its products and across geographies. Currently, the organization's strategic plan is replete with innovative ideas, a focus on growth—both organically and by acquisition—and a new market-facing strategy and expensive campaign. This places a tremendous demand on the senior leadership team to push the culture in the direction of the new strategy. But they have to "take care of business" as they do so. Does this sound familiar? It's a very usual conundrum, but only some teams—the Top Teams—do this well.

In 2007, the Conference Board surveyed 769 CEOs from forty countries (Conference Board 2007). When it asked them to rate their greatest concerns from among 121 different challenges, the vast majority of CEOs chose "excellence of execution" as their number one concern and "keeping consistent execution of strategy by top management" as their third greatest concern.

A wide variety of other research helps to explain why execution has become such an issue for CEOs worldwide: 80 percent to 90 percent of organizations fail to implement effectively what they spend so much time, energy, and money planning. So we see a lot of strong starts but slow or derailed finishes at a time where velocity of execution is critical.

Leland Russell, co-author of *Winning in Fast Time*, and an innovative thinker on execution, says that to win in the New Normal, you must move faster than the rate of change and faster than your competitors (Warden and Russell 2001). In fact, in the vast majority of situations, time is not on your side. *Velocity* is defined in physics as the "rate of change of position along a straight line with respect to time." In other words, velocity includes both doing things at speed and with the proper direction.

As Russell states, "You have be acutely aware of your planning assumptions" (Warden and Russell 2001). No matter how theoretically perfect the original plan may be, as the execution time line lengthens, its value depreciates because the environment (context) changes. You end up executing a plan designed for a world that no longer exists. And be aware of Murphy's Law at work—which states that anything that can go wrong will (go wrong). The longer you take to think, plan, and implement, the greater the chance of unexpected adversity."

In a presentation that Russell and I gave titled "Execution Excellence," we discussed how speed wins in the New Normal because (Levin and Russell 2008):

- Key assumptions don't become obsolete.

- There are fewer unanticipated consequences.

- Internal and external opposition is preempted.

- Execution gaps surface and can be corrected quickly.

- Fast wins create a positive feedback loop.

- The organization's metabolism for action increases.

- Desired results and benefits are accelerated.

There is one caveat here about speed. It's important to know when to move quickly and, equally important, when not to do so because it would be counterproductive. This is difficult for leaders who have to balance the time and depth necessary to think through a complex issue and align their teams behind it with the need for speed. The key is to move at the right speed, which is the speed you need to succeed.

There are eight areas where organizations must succeed in order to execute. To look at this the other way around, there are eight common shortcomings that represent an execution gap:

1. **Failure to ensure that everyone fully understands the "why" behind the change.** The "why" or compelling business reason for any change or new strategy must be clearly articulated to the organization, and to do so, senior teams must understand and buy into it. This is a critical role and responsibility of

the senior or executive teams because they are the ones who must sponsor the change, provide the structure, and assign the resources and time for it. I was recently in a leadership team meeting that was brought to a halt after one of the senior execs rather timidly raised his hand and said, "I'm still not fully clear if this is the right thing to do." The train was about to leave the station, and the rollout of the critical priorities was about to be launched—but if his ambivalence was shared and unspoken by others (and it was), then any strategic work would not have had the energy or direction it needed. So we stopped where we were and talked this through as a team. It is important to have all the issues on, not under, the table as you make this journey.

2. **Failure to engage a critical mass of employees across levels, locations, and functions**. We hear a lot about engagement, but most companies don't know how to do it. They try to "cascade" change by attempting to communicate and get buy-in one level at a time. But this takes a lot of time, and people's day jobs tend to get in the way. The question is: How do you get the right people, across functions, businesses, and distance, to coordinate and engage around the right things in companies that are often highly matrixed and working across geographical boundaries?

3. **Failure to realize that communication is essential, but it's not enough**. Given that the most valuable commodity inside an organization is time, a new way of working utilizing processes and communication platforms that allow many people to work in parallel to drive the priorities forward is required.

4. **Failure to understand the concept of organizational inertia.** This is created by what Leland calls "legacy mindsets and leadership skill gaps," and what Marshall Goldsmith (2007) means with his catchphrase, which is also the title of one of his books, *What Got You Here Won't Get You There.* The New Normal requires a different way of working and thinking about how companies work in more complex and ambiguous environments.

5. **Not having the right tools and processes to maintain transparency and accountability.** By this I mean tools that allow people to work in parallel—globally, virtually, and seamlessly.

6. **Not knowing how to maintain momentum and sustain initiatives over time.** We worked with a large Global 100 company that was implementing a significant growth strategy. A smart and sophisticated company, it still struggled to maintain momentum and sustain good initiatives. What was getting in the way? Life. Business. The day-to-day, quarterly, tactical responsibilities. Deadlines were missed and moved back; momentum was impacted, and it went on. Thus, big change was being derailed and only partially implemented—and the energy and urgency that initially catalyzed the change slipped. Organizations have a long memory over failed initiatives.

7. **Failure to focus resources where they will have maximum impact.** Smart organizations always look at the most essential leverage points on which to focus the critical few initiatives. This is one of the main responsibilities of leaders.

8. **Forgetting the challenge of managing the Now and the New.** This is only last on the list to keep it top in mind. This is an excellent example of paradox management, as we know that leaders have to frequently balance seemingly contradictory approaches where there is not a "right versus wrong" problem. Often it is about balancing two "right" answers. Paradoxes show up with frequency when an emerging strategy meets current reality, and leaders have to know how to operate in a world that is not either/or.

Allowing Optionality and Possibility

The social and behavioral compact with employees is changing as aggressive cost cutting, resource redistribution, opportunistic acquisitions, and so on require people at all levels to acknowledge new realities and operate in ways that can be very different from the past. *Optionality*, as described in Blue Ocean strategy, refers to how the team behaves in ways that maximize its chance to explore options honestly rather than retreating for fear of being wrong or making a mistake (Chan and Mauborgne 2005).

To be anything more than an exercise, optionality within a Top Team setting requires that certain dynamics must be adopted between the team members. First, it must be okay to think together. In most of the surveys and interviews we have done with senior team members, we hear with surprising frequency the desire to think more strategically as a group—to harness the CI and experience of a smart senior team. Often, innovation and forward-thinking strategies are confined to select members of the team or contained within certain functions. For example, the CIO usually has the responsibility for IT, online, web-based solutions. VPs of strategy have the interface with the consultants, futurists, and economists who chart the future. And in the middle of this is often an externally focused CEO, whose job is largely to interface with the external world, leaving the actual running of the organization to a COO (a role which is becoming increasingly rare), a CFO, or a small group of operational direct reports.

Collective intelligence (CI) involves utilizing the entirety of a senior team and, hopefully, the teams that report to them, to bring possibilities to the surface, understand the internal and external worlds, and balance the "real work" of the "Now" and the possibilities of the "New."

Building Confidence and Safety

There are two major dynamics at work—confidence and safety. As one of our pharmaceutical clients said, "In the fierce urgency of the now, you earn the right to implement tomorrow's future by executing today." This is a pretty straightforward statement of how trust is earned in an organization based on executing against the fundamentals of the business.

> "In the fierce urgency of the now, you earn the right to implement tomorrow's future by executing today."

Another client recently said that, "The ticket of admission to thinking strategically around here is being good operationally." This is but one of the dynamics. The willingness to put ideas out there, to ask the "what if" questions, to insert yourself and your ideas into another's area, or to fundamentally question assumptions that are implicit truths, requires a high degree of safety within a team. The bedrock of this is, of course, the trust that is present within a team that is highly aligned, has established clear and well-articulated ground rules about participation, and has a track record of thinking together. Not all new ideas are good ideas. Innovation is a tricky but essential process in a fast-changing and interconnected world. Team members must feel that it is not only their right but also their obligation to think forward.

While there seems to be a desire in many teams to "go back to the basics" of what made a company successful, our view is that while this is important, it is insufficient. The good news about burning platforms is that they create possibility, and the responsibility of senior teams is to recognize, manage, and redirect disruption into focused advantage. This is especially true if we believe, as most do, that periods of crisis and uncertainty end, and organizations with strong leadership teams, good balance sheets, efficient operations, and investments in leadership ultimately prevail.

At the end of the day, the team has to decide on those few, but essential, priorities around which to execute. There is a delicate balance between keeping dialogue open enough to fully explore options and making the decisions around where to sharply focus energy and resources. Knowing the "default setting" of your team—what its preferences are when faced with uncertainty—and ensuring that you lead in such a way as to balance open dialogue with making clear decisions on top priorities are keys to moving optionality to execution.

Questions

THE NOW AND THE NEW

- If time is a valuable commodity for you and your team, when do you find the opportunities to discuss the big issues?

- As leaders, how do you balance your focus on the Now and on the New?

DRIVING THE FIERCE URGENCY OF "NOW":
THE NEED FOR EXECUTION EXCELLENCE

- How would you rate the quality of your execution against your strategic plan? What has happened so far? What must change to make this even more effective?

- What does the concept of "speed" mean in your business and to you personally? Can you and should you accelerate it?

- What obstacles are in the way of executing—with speed—in your company?

- How well has your team/leadership articulated the compelling business reasons behind the changes throughout your company? What has been the result?

- How is the workforce engaged in this process? How could this be improved?

- What venues/opportunities do you have as a leadership team to discuss the "big" issues?

Encouraging and Normalizing Paradox

- How well do you, as a team, identify and discuss important issues that are defined as paradoxes?

- Describe several of the paradoxes you are facing as a management team.

- In your dialogue together, how are these handled? Are they identified as paradoxes to be managed or problems to be solved?

- What are the top two paradoxes that must be fully discussed? What value might come from this discussion?

Allowing Optionality and Possibility

- How well do you, as a leadership team, value and harness your collective intelligence (CI)?

- What would it take to raise the bar? What would be the value?

- In what way do you discuss what is possible and what represents innovation in your business?

- How does innovation get derailed in your company?

Building Confidence and Safety

- How safe is it to challenge fundamental business assumptions? How safe is it to talk about optionality within your team?

- Is the fundamental backdrop of trust present within your team to challenge your performance against the Now and the New?

CHAPTER 4

Wrap Your Head around Change

THE MERGER OF TWO COMPETING *children's hospitals presented significant opportunity to increase the reach and breadth of services to children, drive cutting-edge research from their academic medicine partner, and increase the funding for necessary programs while providing significant reductions in overhead and cost structures. Everyone knew this merger would not be easy given the history of competition between the systems, between physician groups, and between the different cultures. However, it was a necessary move with tremendous upside potential.*

*Predictably, the new hospital leadership team had to align behind the new vision and strategic direction (define what they were **for**) and form as a new team tasked with aligning the stars to bring the combined hospital system together. This was a huge and predictable change for everyone involved. What wasn't* *well-predicted was how difficult this process would be and how, in the face of such great potential, so much overt and passive resistance could be mobilized.*

The senior team needed to address the issue of change in everything it did, said, wrote, or thought. It had to deeply understand the dynamics of the combined organization, honor the histories and cultures of each stakeholder group, create a dynamic and shared vision of a combined structure, articulate the desired behaviors and culture within the new organization, and deal head-on with conflict. This was complex and intense change—not something manageable by a linear seven-step methodology.

The senior team became a Top Team in this journey of understanding and coming together around a well-thought-out change agenda and collectively rising to the responsibilities of providing real leadership within this complex system.

Has Change ... Changed?

It is not the strongest of the species that survive, nor the most intelligent, but the most responsive to change.

—Clarence Darrow (Darrow 1987)

How often have we heard the phrase, attributed to Isaac Asimov, "The only constant is change?" Has the phrase "change" itself become another management cliché—and thus something to be "managed?" Has it become somehow less difficult, unsettling, and disruptive? Or has it become more complex, less predictable, and more ambiguous in nature? A very real question is: Has the nature of change somehow ... changed?

Most models of change are predicated on the belief that change is a disruption to an established pattern or way of doing things. Managing change then, means weathering the storm and managing the process until some degree of normalcy returns. But the return to normalcy hasn't been our experience in some time.

The sudden, intense, global economic shifts that began in 2008 impacted virtually every individual and company across the world. Speed of change and global interconnectedness and interdependence continue to accelerate. We've seen leaders forced to imagine change that would never have been possible or imaginable during their reign, and leaders who are often challenged to fundamentally rethink the very nature of companies they have created, worked at, or led for years. Leadership teams often talk about VUCA—volatility, uncertainty, complexity, and ambiguity—as something they face almost daily. The current Wikipedia definition, which has great face validity, defines the elements of VUCA as: (Wikipedia.org)

- **V** = Volatility: The nature and dynamics of change, and the nature and speed of change forces and change catalysts.

- **U** = Uncertainty: The lack of predictability, the prospects for surprise, and the [difficulty in] awareness and understanding of issues and events.

- **C** = Complexity: The multiplex of forces, the confounding of issues, and the chaos and confusion that surround an organization.

- **A** = Ambiguity: The haziness of reality, the potential for misreads, and the mixed meanings of conditions; cause-and-effect confusion.

Change consultants talk about "waves of change" during which companies and employees experience one disruption after another without returning to solid ground for long periods of time. Neuropsychologists tell us that the human brain is not evolutionally developed to deal with constant change. Our amygdala tells us to flee, fight, or freeze in response to threats, with a return to homeostasis as an eventual experience. That is, until the next event. These neuropsychologists make the point that we are not wired for constant disruption or "flooding."

In today's world, the frequent waves of change, high volatility and complexity, and significant paradox and ambiguity create a whitewater experience. This experience creates huge paradigm shifts for executives and employees alike as the very ground underneath them feels shaky. This brings to mind questions such as: "How do we deal with the Now and the New?" "What is the New Normal?" "Does the New Normal somehow represent continuous, complex, ambiguous, and uncertain change, like a river that is truly never the same?" Our thinking is that the very nature of change has been altered on both a personal and a business level. Change has changed. And Top Teams do a far better job in wrapping their heads around change than do merely good teams. What makes the difference?

Models of Change: What Works in the New Normal

There are many models in the popular literature that describe how to take an organization through the necessary steps to "manage change." John Kotter has his widely used 8-Step Process. (Kotter 1996) There are three-step, five-step and ten-step models. Some models purport to manage all kinds of change; others more narrowly focus on accelerating the implementation of complex projects such as a new SAP (systems applications and products) system. Virtually every leadership development program has a "module" on change. Knock yourselves out.

Those of us who have seen change—big change—either driven by or happening to senior teams know that while there are some good guidelines out there, there are also no road maps that apply to your unique business at this unique time in history. There is no linear process that applies equally. There are no "five easy steps to neurosurgery." Therefore, senior teams must "wrap their heads around change," by understanding the very nature of change—how each change deeply impacts their organizations and relates to their strategy, what the role of the leaders must be, and what must be done to have a prayer of success. Great teams must do a great job in understanding the dynamics and actions to be good at this. You cannot copycat change, and you can't do it in ten easy steps.

In his impressive book *Champions of Change,* David Nadler describes a model of change characterized by increased "intensity and complexity," which he refers to as "discontinuous change." (Nadler 1998) *Discontinuous change* is an intense, complex, and often destabilizing type of change caused by responses to anticipated or current crises. Discontinuous change, in contrast to "incremental change," which is far less intense and more predictable, requires far greater involvement of and direction by the senior leadership team. Nadler asks, "Can you recognize the changes that are about to happen early enough to develop a sufficient response? Can you make the right strategic choices that will allow your organization to survive or profit from this period of disequilibrium? Are you capable of reshaping or redesigning essential parts of your organization to implement a new strategic direction?" (Nadler 1998)

Nadler's is a nonlinear and well-reasoned approach to the kinds of change we are seeing today, which require leadership teams to set a change agenda based on a clear view of the desired future. Through focused dialogue, these teams must determine what they are *for*, then align behind the critical priorities and collectively drive the organization toward the New while managing the responsibilities needed in the Now.

Optimizing Control and Predictability: Taking Care of You and Them

Leading change requires maximizing a sense of predictability and control, especially when both feel in short supply. Predictability and control are the two major variables that impact how people experience stress. If people experience a lack of predictability in which they feel blindsided by or uncertain about the future, and also experience low control over what is occurring to them, the classic response is one of high stress. The disruption caused by this stress is both corrosive to individuals and distracting to the organization.

> "Leading change requires maximizing a sense of predictability and control, especially when both feel in short supply."

Because the ambiguity and complexity of today's change is continuously on the forefront today, open and proactive communication about what will and must change is essential. Giving people as much control as possible over their own destinies is essential. Providing them with as much information as possible about the external forces that are likely to impact them, and then engaging them to create maximum internal readiness (options), drives their engagement in the process. It is equally important to communicate what will *not* change in organizations. Core values, operational excellence, uncompromising safety, and authenticity are among those things that, for great companies, should not change. The research on "old" companies, those that have lasted fifty years or more, indicates that core values hold true over time and withstand the winds of change.

One of the leaders we interviewed compared being in the midst of change to halftime in a football game. During halftime, the coaches spend time talking about what has happened thus far, but they focus on the top priorities for the second half and the need to execute against these. This focus drives predictability and control, and diminishes the disruption that is corrosive to performance. Leaders have a tremendous responsibility to do the same, coaching their players and their teams when uncertainty abounds and threat seems to be around the corner.

Be Visible and Talk Straight

There is no more important time for leaders to be visible than when in the midst of change. A CEO of a large life-sciences firm told us that if people are paying attention to just the headlines, they'll become distracted and driven by fear. This, he said, is antithetical to building the alignment, collaboration, and trust in leadership that are so critical to have at this moment in time.

Building and maintaining trust is primary, yet difficult to earn and keep during these times. A scarcity mentality breeds bad behaviors. People tend to become more siloed and more tribal when feeling threatened. After restructurings have taken place in already lean organizations, people must do more with fewer resources, with more pressure and less certainty. There is likely an imbalance of loyalty, as the employees sense that they care more about the organization than management cares about them.

Yet, paradoxically, this becomes the time when both leaders and staff have to reach across functions and geographies and be more collaborative. Lack of trust slows things down at a time when speed is of the essence. Leadership teams must pay attention to those things that engender and build trust—ensuring there is a good balance between "say" and "do."

Clearly, the responsibility of leadership teams is to build this trust, communicate clearly, engage employees to assist in solving problems, and be as honest and transparent as possible—to their customers, employees, stakeholders, and one another. It is a critical time to remind the organization what it is *for*, and what must be done in the Now.

Never Waste a Good Crisis

When you change the way you look at things, the things you look at change.

—Max Planck

We talked earlier about the waypoints that good teams must navigate on their journey to becoming great teams—Top Teams. We know from studies of physics, chemistry, politics, and psychology that the advancement of human behavior does not happen in a straight line. As a metaphor, the Army Corps of Engineers has for many years been attempting to straighten out the mighty Mississippi River, which has an annoying habit of meandering—thus changing shipping channels, riverbanks, and sandbars. Their success has been limited and, in the grand scheme of such things, short-term. In the 1980s a physics student studying the properties of water found that he could not get a single drop of water to move in a straight line down a pane of glass and concluded that the essential nature of water is to meander. As the saying goes, there are no straight lines in nature.

And there are no straight lines in the art and practice of leadership. It is in the constant journey of leaders and the learning that occurs through dialogue and correction that great teams get it mostly right. Tugboat captains do a better job on the river than engineers. They have the pattern intelligence that comes with navigating an organic and ever-changing system and the necessary willingness to constantly adjust to their environment. Thus it is with setting and following strategy in a flexible and movable environment. Flexibility wins, and dialogue is the currency of the land.

To use an American football analogy (often confusing to followers of real "football," known as soccer here in the United States), a good quarterback has a play (a plan) in mind, and every player knows his role and route, but the defense (the external environment) is set up to thwart the play. The good quarterback calls an "audible"—a change that adjusts the play to respond immediately to the defensive scheme, thus changing the assignments for individual players and the collective team. Great teams call audibles with great frequency. Their experience and agility allow them to see patterns in the external environment and quickly adjust.

> "It is in the constant journey of leaders and the learning that occurs through dialogue and correction that great teams get it mostly right."

Top Teams see the opportunities inherent in change and adjust their strategies accordingly. Over the course of the last few years, we interviewed dozens of senior leaders across a variety of industries and were surprised by their excitement and confidence in seeing the opportunities that existed as the markets and economic conditions shifted around them. As one VP of finance suggested, "Burning platforms create opportunities, but it is the responsibility of this team to manage the disruption and find the value." Another leader told us that this was the time where she really earned her money—that if she was not able to lead in these turbulent times, than she had no right to call herself a leader.

Yet, separating the professional from the personal is more difficult than ever as many senior people see their net worth, options, and retirement plans under water with less sense of the old reference points. As Dr. Patricia Wheeler has commented, "It's like working without handholds. Where is the old normal to hang onto as you are creating the New Normal?" (Wheeler personal conversation) How do leaders lead change while in the middle of it themselves?

Clearly, the responsibility of leadership teams is to build this trust, communicate clearly, engage employees to assist in solving problems, and be as honest and transparent as possible—to their customers, employees, stakeholders, and one another.

Questions

HAS CHANGE ... CHANGED?

- How has the nature of change changed for you?

- What have been some of the most significant changes to impact your business in the past three years?

- What have been some of the most disruptive changes to you in that time?

- Describe where you see increased VUCA (volatility, uncertainty, complexity, and ambiguity) in your world and within your organization.

- What has been the impact on you and on other leaders?

- How well is your team talking about and handling the changes that you describe?

- What could you do even better?

Models of Change: What Works in the New Normal?

- How thoroughly have you and your team talked about those changes that impact you?

- How well do you understand the dynamics and potential impact of change on your team and on the workforce?

- Do you have a model of change that you follow?

- Do you deliberately try to predict what may occur and prepare alternatives?

- How able and agile is your company in responding to unexpected changes?

Optimizing Control and Predictability: Taking Care of You and Them

- How proactive are you with your workforce in discussing potential and possible disruptive change? Do you normalize it?

- How involved and engaged are they in crafting responses to changes?

- Do you remind them about what is *not* changing in the company?

- Do you actively coach your players about how best to respond to VUCA?

BE VISIBLE AND TALK STRAIGHT

- What are you doing to ensure clear communication with the workforce?

- How do you know how they are responding and their view of leadership?

- Where could you be even more proactive and communicative?

NEVER WASTE A GOOD CRISIS

- In what ways have you utilized these complex and uncertain times to build opportunities for your business? How have you used the "burning platform" for change?

- How have you grown as a leader?

CHAPTER 5
Essential Navigational Skills

ONE OF OUR MOST CHALLENGED *clients was a well-established, conservative pharmaceutical company that was in the process of acquiring a smaller, entrepreneurial, fast-moving European firm. While our client was used to working in the global arena and had methodically made acquisitions to foster manufacturing capabilities, open new markets, and bring additional discovery online, they had little experience in bringing onboard senior talent who operated differently. Founders and leaders of the smaller firm were more informal, results-driven, urgent, and usually harder working than the larger company. They were certainly less bureaucratic, were process-oriented, and were immediately frustrated by the "realities" of the larger organization.*

In the course of interviews with all the parties, one of the acquirees made the statement, "It is interesting to watch a team justify why certain realities are what they are. We don't operate that way." For the acquirees, this was a case of justifying current and historical ways of operating that served to slow the fast movers down. But in the eyes of the acquirer, the smaller company was doing the same thing in reverse—justifying why their reality was right.

*The challenge was to align the combined organization behind what it was **for** (why the deal was done in the first place) and to inform both parties about how the collision between "vision and reality" was going to damage what was possible.*

Making the Complex Understandable

If you can't make sense of it quickly at the top, the ability for it to make sense one or two levels down the organization is impossible.

—Iain Melville, CEO, RCD
(Melville personal conversation)

One of the most important attributes of the leader of a Top Team is to be able to make the complex understandable to the next levels of the workforce. This statement may be obvious, but it is much more difficult to do than it sounds. In previous chapters, we discussed how complex, volatile, and ambiguous the business world is, and how fast things change. And this is the external context within which clear strategy and a compelling sense of purpose—how an organization defines what it is *for* and what drives alignment within it—must exist. In the crucible that is a Top Team, one key responsibility is to make what is complex understandable to everyone in the organization on a continuing basis even as the business evolves. As Irial Finan (personal conversation) of Coca Cola's Bottling Investment Group states with characteristic clarity, "Leaders here must be able to manage complex issues simultaneously."

This is no easy task. Sometimes making the complex understandable is to provide a clear summary of where the organization is heading and how it is changing or adapting to external forces. Often it involves communicating the two or three critical priorities that people have to accomplish and what their functional accountability looks like. But two things are always true:

1. The horizon of strategic thinking is continuing to shrink, and

2. if the team at the top is unsure, uncertain, or vague about the strategic direction of the organization, then those fault lines will spread deep and wide across the company.

Many CEOs and chief strategy officers will say that a three- to five-year strategy, at one point a norm for companies, is now unrealistic. Many say that an eighteen-month window is a stretch. This is why having a strong compass heading, i.e., understanding clearly the direction, focus, and values of the organization, may serve as "true north." Breaking this down to more operational terms, leadership teams may then use this heading with a rolling three-year goal process that is examined and adjusted every year or, in the case of companies that operate in a more turbulent space, every three months. The major point here is that strategy has to be "directionally correct" and operational planning has to be clear.

One important observation that has held true across industry teams is that leaders and senior managers who sit on senior teams always know if something about the strategy is unclear. Yet, they rarely say it if it seems to contradict the CEO or an already established (and unconfronted) strategy. You often hear, "We already decided that," or "Where were you when this discussion took place?" This is an easy way to shut down dialogue, to be sure. But as we look to raise the bar of a senior team and to ensure that alignment around critical priorities occurs, champions arise in unusual places.

We had a long-standing relationship with a large construction company and had worked closely with them through both significant growth periods and some economic downturns. Construction companies, for the uninitiated, are very sophisticated around teamwork. Each project they build is different from the one before, and it is built by a diverse group of people representing different specialties that must come together and form a seamless team. This team must succeed while facing high risk, low margins, tight schedules, and complex problems that involve numerous companies (subcontractors) and many workers. They have to make many ongoing decisions and be skilled at identifying and resolving issues quickly.

In the midst of a senior team meeting that was focused on when to open an office in Las Vegas, Bob, one of the grizzled veterans, raised his hand and asked how this investment contributed to the strategy of the company going forward and how it served the business case given the current economic climate. The CEO, a pretty tough guy in his own right, brushed past the question, stating that they had already talked about this and that, "This train has already left the station." Most people would have given up, but Bob stuck to his guns and continued, "I still don't understand why we are doing this …"

What typically happens in such a situation? The CEO acknowledges the question but moves on, much like what happened within this meeting. Or, the questioner gives up and "acts like a team player," thereby depriving the leadership team of a chance to look at a decision with Bob's viewpoint in mind.

The best option for the CEO and the senior team is to ask Bob to state his case and lay out his concerns. Their responsibility at this point is to listen, really listen, not just to push Bob to move on, but to be informed by his questions and concerns. This dynamic accomplishes at least three things that are essential for the team:

1. Bob may have a point that is in their enlightened collective interest;

2. they demonstrate their commitment to dialogue and alignment among the senior team; and

3. they get to keep Bob as a full contributor within the team.

How many times have you seen people give up because they feel their opinion is devalued? And how often have you seen a decision made where agreement is not real? As a partner of mine, Boyce Appel (personal conversation), used to say, "Silence is not assent."

Deciding How to Decide

We've talked about the need to articulate the senior purpose of a team—what the team is truly *for*. At the highest individual and collective levels, it is about defining the one or two collective and "audacious" goals that far exceed the individual goals of the individual leaders. It is about how to prioritize the *New*—the critical and essential priorities and investments the senior team must make to achieve its future—and it is also about how to deal with the *Now*—the priorities and variables of today. But there are many decisions that are unexpected and surprising—many of them urgent in nature. Many leadership teams are at their best in the emergency or fire-fighting mode, but they struggle to stay on track and keep their eyes on the larger prize in the day-to-day work or in harnessing the Collective Intelligence to make great decisions about the future.

Making good decisions involves having an agreed-upon process designed to remove much of the confusion and noise. One fundamental observation of Top Teams is that they understand that different situations require different methods of making decisions. And they have worked out the "rules of the road" about how they operate.

Simplistically, there are five ways of making a decision on a senior team:

1. The CEO (or person in charge) unilaterally makes the call.

2. The person in charge makes the call with the input of the team (or key members).

3. The team makes the decision by consensus.

4. The team requires unanimity.

5. The team votes.

Given five (or more) choices, how does a team know which method to use? The answer is found in a simple process known as "labeling," which states that "the CEO (or person in charge) 'labels' the process that is most appropriate to the decision at hand." In other words, the decision process is situational but clearly understood. And, while there is no one right way of doing this, sometimes the process is apparent.

Four years ago, I was on an airplane from Atlanta to San Francisco when the pilot informed us that we had lost an engine and were diverting to St. Louis. Noticeably, he did not come into the cabin and ask, "How many people want to try and make it to San Francisco?" It was an emergency situation, and he made the call he was paid to make. Likewise, a CEO should make those calls that are immediate, or of a certain nature that it is uniquely hers/his to make. This decision is labeled "The CEO (or person in charge) unilaterally makes the call." The team understands the circumstances that require the CEO's immediate decision and in which situations this occurs.

An important thing to remember is that if the CEO (or person in charge) overuses this style (which he or she does have the organizational clout to do), the team reduces its level of engagement and team members become mere order takers. This is seen in classic command-and-control organizations, in which team members are tasked to execute against their promises and numbers. But in an emergency or urgency situation, fast and informed decisions are required.

A number of years ago, I was asked to consult with a chemical plant, which was trying, unsuccessfully, to move to a self-directed type of decision-making designed to reduce the traditional hierarchy of boss-employer relationships. Their experienced supervisors' roles had been minimized, and, in an optimistic attempt to create a more democratic and engaged workforce, the inmates took over running the asylum. This was mostly fine until an emergency occurred. At 3:00 a.m. on the third shift, alarm Klaxons began to sound and red lights started to flash. We were in a chemical plant that was potentially explosive and very dangerous. And we were in trouble. Workers began to shout over one another and the scene became highly disorganized and frenetic as numerous people tried to make decisions that were, at best, complex and highly choreographed. The situation went from bad to worse as more sirens began to wail across the plant. People (including me) were scared—appropriately so. Fred, a long-term and highly experienced supervisor, was leaning against the wall with people imploring him to do something. After sarcastically asking whether his directives would interfere with their being "self-directed," he said, "Okay, I am in charge—this is what we'll do," and he issued a series of orders that effectively scrammed (shut down) the plant. We spent the next several days debriefing the team on the emergency and decision-making processes that had occurred. As a side note, the self-directed teamwork, while well-intentioned, was scrapped. This is a clear example of when an intended decision-making format—consensus—was not appropriate to the situation at hand. But it may have worked well on a more day-to-day routine. Like many things, strength when taken to excess becomes weakness. Using just one decision-making style across all circumstances doesn't work.

A second decision style is to "have the person in charge (PIC) make the call with the input of the team (or key members)." This is an informed decision-making process in which members of the team are asked for their opinions and best decisions, clearly knowing that the PIC will make the call *after* hearing from each of the key people. But to do this well involves more than just listening to others or even doing the classic "listening check" to ensure that message sent was message heard. The critical ingredient in this style is to let members of the team know how what they said informed the decision and what the PIC learned from their input. Again, we are talking in the context of alignment within a Top Team, which has, at its core, leaders who are highly engaged and "all-in."

Again, when this style is overused or not clearly understood, weaknesses can appear. To the extent team members think that their opinions are not taken into account, they may check out of future dialogue wondering, "Why does he even ask this question of me if he's not going to use my input?" This input-based PIC decision process is powerful and has, at its highest and best, the advantage of fast and high-quality decisions with fewer opportunities to have a blind spot.

The third style, "the team makes the decision by consensus," is powerful, but often misused and misunderstood. At best it is the organic result of dialogue, after which the team realizes it has reached a decision that is agreed-to by most, if not all, members. Nearly everyone is nodding. But there are two key rules in consensual decision-making. Rule #1 is "No dead body rule." This means that no one can internally mutter, "This will happen over my dead body," even if that person is just one voice in the group. If anybody feels this strongly, the articulated agreement is that this person sticks to his or her guns until or unless he or she can convince the group to change its mind or, more likely, he or she feels heard and can live with the decision. This dialogue makes the group smarter and more aligned. And that takes us to Rule #2, which is a working and agreed-upon definition of *consensus*: "Even if I don't love this decision, I can live with and support it—in public and in private." This last part is essential, as public support but private criticism is toxic to a team and produces fault lines down the organization. It also can become a question of integrity, which is one of the few stand-alone behavioral issues that can cause a team member to lose his or her place on the team. Consensus can be viewed as a weak or a strong decision, depending on the energy and engagement with which it is made.

> "A working and agreed-upon definition of *consensus*: "Even if I don't love this decision I can live with and support it—in public and in private."

A fourth decision process is "the team requires unanimity." Everybody has to agree for this one to work. Unanimous decisions sound good but, unless they happen organically, can take forever. The upside is high agreement; the downside is the long process that is involved to reach unanimity and the fact that any team member can blackball a decision. One of the few areas where unanimity makes sense is when a small team has to choose someone to join that team.

A fifth way of making decisions, which may be the least favored, is "the team votes." Voting produces winners and losers and often sets dynamics in play that deeply interfere with alignment and sustainability of decisions over time. Straw voting is sometimes helpful to sample opinion and to drive dialogue forward. But at a senior team level, the United States Supreme Court not included, voting can disenfranchise members.

Again, the key point here is that decision-making is situational, and good leaders "label" how each decision should be made. Top Teams make complex decisions about the Now and the New, and they do so with a good understanding of the rules of the game.

There is much written about decision-making (seventy-eight million hits on Google at the time of this writing, and, no, I didn't read them all), but the key point is how critical it is to agree on a process that *really* works, defined as high-quality decisions, made at speed, with strong engagement from the senior team.

Navigating the Formal and Informal Organizations

One of the tried and true adages is that "when culture and change collide, culture always wins." For those of us who are, or who have been, change agents or tasked to sponsor a change of any size, we quickly learn that an essential skill is being able to navigate the organization—both the formal structure and the informal network. One shorthand definition of culture is that it is composed of the vision of the organization—what the company says it stands for, the policies and procedures that support that direction and influence behavior—and the norms of the company—how it really works on the shop floor, in other words, the informal organization.

Imagine that you have interviewed for a job. You've done your research and have met a senior VP, who tells you great things about the company. You next go to HR, who, in addition to welcoming you aboard, tells you about policies, incentive compensation, and the do's and don'ts of the place. Then you go to work—hopefully optimistically. A co-worker named Fred introduces himself and asks if you've met the SVP and the HR person. He then says, "Let me tell you how it really works around here." He points to the manager and tells you what you have to do to succeed with him. He tells you about the people on your team—and how they operate together. If you are fortunate, what he tells you matches what you heard in your orientation. But what you may well hear is that the informal organization, its norms and behaviors, operate somewhat differently than the formal organization would indicate. In the best of worlds, the vision, policies, and norms line up. But in many cases, they do not.

From a leadership perspective, being able to navigate both the formal and informal organizations is essential, but involves somewhat different skills. Often, the formal organization is more political, the decision rights are more structured, the lines of reporting are better defined, and the navigation is somewhat more cautious. The informal organization is all about relationships and credibility. It requires walking around, asking questions, listening well, living your professed values, and walking the talk. Leaders who are not in touch with the informal organization often fail slowly, as the collective can take passive resistance to the level of an art form, thus effectively killing new programs, slowing down adoption of changes, and frustrating leaders who are not in touch.

Top Teams understand the criticality of dealing with both

the formal and the informal organization—the top business and functional leaders, the board of directors, and, when applicable, the street. They are in touch with the pulse of the company and work consciously and deliberately to build relationships with work groups across geographies and functional areas. They check their work by using good engagement and opinion surveys, town hall meetings, luncheons, and one-to-one meetings to ask questions and listen. Finally, they follow up on what they hear, thus building credibility and trust.

Engagement: Waxing the Forklift

The best plant manager I have ever known was Norm Kuhl at Coors Brewing. Some time ago, Norm was asked to reopen a plant that, at one point, had been a competitors' factory, with the former plant's union workforce and contracts intact. The workforce was suspicious of new management, and new management was inheriting a workforce that it did not know, in a city it did not know. There were no shortages of concerns on both sides as the cultures were unfamiliar with each other.

Very early on, Norm stated that the goal of the management team members was to earn the respect of the workforce by demonstrating respect for them. To do this, they had to earn the trust of the union and create a culture that was clear about its values, its behaviors, and its direction (what it was *for*). And it had to walk that talk. We worked closely with the management team to define the behavioral rules and the operating agreements within the team and between management and the workforce. Listening was a prized skill—something unfamiliar to workers. Trust, in the form of making and keeping agreements, was essential. Defining a common future was, at the time, almost a radical idea—one that was met with equal parts promise and skepticism.

About nine months later, I was taking a tour of the plant with Norm (who seemed to know each worker by name). We came upon a forklift operator who was carefully waxing his forklift. Norm asked him, "Ralph, why are you waxing that forklift?" Ralph unforgettably replied, "Mr. Kuhl, I am proud of this job and want to show it." Norm winked at me. So what happened in a factory that had a history of labor/management distrust in a tough city that produced a lot of rough guys? It began with a management team that was aligned in its view and in its behaviors. The team remained constant, focused, and respectful through issues and conflict. And its consistent messaging about what was possible together—the "Brightness and Darkness of the Future," aligned and engaged the workforce.

Responsibility: The Real Story

Good management and leadership teams bring extraordinary influence to the organization, beginning with the decisions they make as a team and the consistency with which they walk the talk. We talked earlier about how critical it is to define what a team is *for* as a way of setting a direction that provides a common view of a desired future. The leadership team also sets the *culture*, which can simplistically be defined as the vision of an organization, those behaviors that are prized (and the policies that support them), and sets how the informal organization works. To the extent that there is a gap between what is prized and how a firm works, there is tension, suspicion, and a suboptimization of what is possible.

Many years ago, in the sprawling, incredibly diverse, and wonderful Dekalb Farmers' Market in Atlanta, Georgia, I noticed a man wearing the yellow gloves and white apron of the seafood department stop to pick up a piece of lettuce that was on the floor of the warehouse. I asked him why he had done that, and he simply said, "Because I am responsible." Think about that. The Farmers' Market has virtually every culture, language, and country of origin represented, and it works. When I interviewed members of the management team and told them of my experience, they responded that they were clear and consistent about the behaviors that they prized and how these behaviors contributed to the overall linking vision of the enterprise. Everyone can tie her or his personal goals to this larger picture and, thus, be responsible for the market's success. And it remains true to this day.

An old model of responsibility, which I learned in my earliest consulting days at the Atlanta Consulting Group, was the 100 percent responsibility model. When asked, most people would say that when you and another person have to get something done, you each have to be 50 percent responsible for the outcome. However, if people fail to get the results, what occurs? Blame for the other and justification of our own behavior. Did the intended results occur? Clearly not. A more enlightened model is the 100-100 model, in which each person takes 100 percent of the responsibility. If the results do not occur, you get a more sophisticated form of blaming. This leads to what has always been a radical but thought-provoking model, which is the 100-0 model. This asks the question, "If I am 100 percent responsible for the outcome and everybody and everything else is 0 percent responsible, what can I do (or in retrospect, what could I have done)?" This produces a no-excuses way of looking at responsibility. Is it completely realistic? Probably not. But it gets our attention with no filters, no blaming, and no justifying. Try it.

Questions

MAKING THE COMPLEX UNDERSTANDABLE

- How crisp and clear is your going-forward strategy?

- Is it clearly understood by all members of your senior team?

- How well is it understood by the workforce? Do they get both the expectations of the Now and the strategy for the New?

- How well can people link their roles to the critical priorities for the organization?

DECIDING HOW TO DECIDE

- How quickly and accurately do you make decisions within your team?

- Do you have an agreed-upon decision-making model in place?

- On a scale of one to ten, rate the quality and speed of your decision process. What would it take to be a ten?

- Do you "label" how each decision will be made?

NAVIGATING THE FORMAL AND INFORMAL ORGANIZATIONS

- How do you define the "formal organization" in your company?

- How does it work? What are the spoken and unspoken rules?

- How in touch are you with the "informal organization?" How do you know?

- In what way does the informal organization "push back"? Who are the key influencers within the informal organization?

ENGAGEMENT: WAXING THE FORKLIFT

- How do you measure the engagement of your workforce against your critical priorities?

- How well do what the formal organization says and what the informal organization does match up?

- Do you have behavioral ground rules that people understand and follow?

RESPONSIBILITY: THE REAL STORY

- What is your definition of "responsibility"?

- What is the limitation of believing that you and another each have 50 percent of the responsibility for an outcome?

- Think of a situation that you approach as if you are 100 percent responsible for the outcome and everything and everybody else is 0 percent responsible. What changes as a result? How difficult is it?

CHAPTER 6

The Art of the Advance: How Good Teams Get Even Better

BEING A "C-LEVEL" PLAYER HAS never been more difficult. Major changes in the marketplace, increased competition, and the ability to recruit and retain top talent are among the most daunting challenges facing executive leadership. The balancing act of increasing competitive advantage while decreasing risk, of managing growth while "bottom-proofing" the company, and of maintaining the culture and community of a firm while moving it into the future is a difficult, yet essential, process to manage.

Yet, while successful firms acknowledge the need for tremendous teamwork, most executive teams do not excel in open, high-order dialogue with one another—even when stakes are high and change is rampant. It is not unusual for executive management meetings to be characterized by careful, deliberate presentations or report-out formats that are so well-polished that real issues never surface.

It is a cliché to say that it is lonely at the top, but it is a cliché that is true. Who does the CEO or president talk to? Senior teams are stocked with experience and talent, but most CEOs do not utilize this skill base or leverage the loyalty formed from working closely together for many years. Who do members of a senior team confide in? While meetings at an executive level occur frequently, powerful, honest, and open dialogue is rare.

The Need for High-Order Dialogue

Dialogue literally means an exchange of ideas. Effective dialogue is essential to produce the strategic thinking and implementation that create unique competitive advantage.

Why is good dialogue so difficult for many competent, experienced executives?

There are four reasons:

1. Culture is a shadow of CEO style: Many organizations have a structure in which one person is the dominant force, sometimes the major owner, of the company. Often, the culture of a firm is the shadow of the CEO's style. It is normal for those at the next level, even the most senior level, to treat that CEO or executive with respect and diffidence.

   At worst, a CEO can surround himself or herself with "yes people"—sycophants whose function is to agree at the surface level and carry out the wishes emanating from the top. This creates huge blind spots in any organization and leads to a culture of public agreement and private complaining. This makes for bad strategy, bad morale, and bad decisions, and ultimately drives talented and ambitious managers underground or out of the firm. Great companies thrive on a delicate balance between respect for leadership and individual empowerment. An aligned senior team provides the model for how culture works—what behaviors are reinforced and what behaviors are extinguished by the organization.

True alignment only occurs if people feel able to shoot straight, differ publicly, raise different ideas, and dialogue fully. This ability is based on building a solid and trusting team. Being careful does not work. But being straight is not easy or without risk.

2. Old habits die hard: Senior meetings have a form and rhythm based on history, culture, and habits. In our work, we observe many different teams in operation. When asked to rate the quality of a meeting and whether it accomplished its real objectives, participants can tell you what is working as advertised and what is not productive. But this clarity is usually post hoc and rarely leads to more open and useful time together. How often do you step back and ask your group whether you are dealing with the issues at hand during your time together?

A common phrase we hear is, "It's the way we've always done it." Since old habits are hard to break, a shift in focus and approach is required to create effective dialogue.

Unfortunately, the impetus for this type of change is often some calamity or threat to the organization which demonstrates that business as usual is not working. Pain is highly motivating. It is the "burning platform" that fosters change. But pain is costly and promotes reactive decisions. Neither does it produce sustained behavior change, as people return to their comfort zones when the threat goes away.

3. What if it gets worse? A common fear is that open dialogue creates conflict or can worsen simmering problems. Many groups choose to keep a lid on issues that are commonly known but unexpressed. This only serves to keep problems covert and unresolved.

4. It is certainly difficult to confront peers about their performance or their behavior. It is even more difficult to confront the boss, especially if he or she is the owner of the firm. Organizations have stories, myths, and legends about the tragic consequences of confronting a boss.

Several years ago, a powerful and feared CEO of a large firm told me that he could not confide in, and therefore could not trust, any of his direct reports. When I asked him why, he responded, "They are all afraid of me." While he was sophisticated enough to know the cost of avoidance to the organization, he did not know how to break the pattern. It took a series of executive "Advances" in which we dealt directly with the dynamics of the management team—what the CEO needed and expected from them, and what he did to engender their fear—before they were able to begin to talk candidly with one another. He also, much to their surprise, asked for feedback on his effectiveness. It was only then that the talented players on this team could align to solve the imminent problems facing the company, make hard decisions together, and create a strategy to move the company forward.

From a cost-benefit perspective, the cost to the company of not having the benefit of effective dialogue among the senior team was enormous. Critical problems were unexpressed and unresolved, opportunities could not be realized, poor morale created a revolving-door atmosphere, and the company could not be agile or creative. The benefits of dialogue were impressive: the team was able to bottom-proof the organization and withstand market changes, execute a critical acquisition, and restructure management with a company-wide view to anticipate new markets. As a result, the team has been able to sustain growth in volume, profitability, and talent over the past five years.

Leadership sets the tone for either candor or carefulness. Unresolved issues limit an executive team and restrict what is possible for the company. *If you cannot talk about it, how can you address it and continually improve?*

This is not an easy dilemma to solve. It falls outside the usual skill set for a firm whose leaders have evolved through operations, technical expertise, business acumen, and hard work. Most leaders have terrific strategic and content knowledge. But unless they trust their senior team and their direct reports to fully understand the risks and critical company issues, leaders often stay "in the weeds," not at the twenty-thousand-foot level they should occupy.

How does leadership improve their ability to truly engage issues and create effective dialogue? What is the ROI (return on investment) from addressing these critical activities? What must happen to align the stars and create teamwork among the skilled players on the senior team?

Differentiating an Advance from a Retreat

Leadership teams at all levels have a lot of meetings; many, if not most, of them important and necessary. Some are operational, report-out meetings that measure biweekly or quarterly performance against targets and allow the tactical shifts necessary to make the numbers, address issues that arise, and foster enough operational agility to confront changes in the external and internal environments. Other meetings are briefings—information exchanges designed to keep everyone on the same page about enterprise and organizational shifts. There is no shortage of meetings in corporate America.

The "Advance" meeting is a different sort of animal. It is dialogue-driven, strategically focused, and often quite personal. We call it an Advance for a reason: It is focused on the Now and the New—on the powerful present and the ever-present future. It is relevant, pragmatic, and honest. It is an exercise in aligning and utilizing the CI of the senior team. And given that the most precious commodity of senior leaders is time, an Advance has to be thought of as something different—as essential and unique.

> "If you cannot talk about it, how can you address it and continually improve?"

The Advance is lightly agenda-driven, so the direction of the meeting follows what is most important to talk about and is steered by the energy in the room. It begins by asking the question, "What, if anything, has changed, and how does that impact our strategic direction and critical priorities?" This question is especially important in this time of increased complexity, speed of change, and global connectedness.

> "An Advance has to be thought of as something different—as essential, and unique."

Our bias is that any Advance of one or two days should contain several essential components that deserve honest dialogue:

1. A thorough exploration or confirmation of the company or divisional strategy. What, if anything, has changed? How does this impact the team's priorities?

2. Dialogue about any issues that must be addressed and resolved. This can involve deep discussion about team dynamics; matters of structure, turf, and collaboration; and issues between team members. Silence is not an option and never constitutes agreement.

3. Dialogue about how people are working as a team. What are they doing well, and what can they do to raise the bar? Dialogue about the organization's teams—how are they collaborating and operating together one to three levels down? And how can this be even better?

4. Dialogue about growth and innovation. What possibilities and options exist? What is going on with competitors and out there in the bigger world?

5. How can senior team members improve as individual leaders? This is an opportunity for leadership development, both individually and collectively, and is absolutely a critical question to ask.

6. How do senior team members develop and grow their teams and people? This is a key area, as increased collaboration and competency one and two levels down free up the senior team to be more strategic and to think together.

7. And lastly and always—an after action review (AAR) that measures the quality of the meeting and assesses how to raise the bar over time.

This Advance should be thought of as special time and should be held off-site, every quarter. Teams that are in significant change, new teams, and teams with new leadership may require more frequent meetings. It is a mandatory meeting, with clear and agreed rules of the road about participation, listening, confidentiality, and distractions. The key here is open and honest dialogue about the stuff that matters most.

> "Silence is not an option and never constitutes agreement."

Seven variables differentiate an Advance from a common Retreat.

1. When culture and change collide ... culture usually wins. To change a senior team's culture, you must change its operating behaviors and norms. *Culture* is loosely defined as the combination of values, policies, and norms within an organization. If there is a lack of alignment between any of these three areas, conflict will arise. Companies talk about culture all the time, but it is rarely examined consciously and deliberately, especially at the executive level.

   The executive "Advance" must explore the company's culture—its norms, what gets reinforced, and what the executive team models. Behavior must be changed at the top—among the senior group—before the rest of the firm will follow.

   When senior leadership preaches or prioritizes change, no matter how essential it may be to the company, the employee body watches how it operates and what its track record has been before they buy in and implement new behavior. Organizations of all sizes and shapes regale us with stories of good ideas that were not executed and of great strategies that were poorly implemented. This is expensive in many ways, including the loss of credibility and faith in management.

If culture is unexamined, change, no matter how critical, cannot be sustained. A focused and deliberate Advance is a powerful environment for surfacing old behaviors and creating a flexible, adaptive, and competitive culture. Established culture always beats change.

2. The moose is loose: The ability to, as Sidney Taurel of Eli Lilly is reported to have said "put the moose on the table" and talk openly about difficult issues differentiates an Advance from a typical planning session. Total candor and productive dialogue about difficult issues have a major impact on trust and how well an executive team operates.

As teams get more used to dealing directly with one another, tough issues are surfaced with greater confidence. A great quote that applies here is attributed to Buckminster Fuller, "Not getting it is what takes the time." To the extent that tough issues are dealt with successfully and a track record is established, the "moose" gets smaller, shows up less frequently, and doesn't smell quite as bad.

3. Focus on process as well as content: An Advance focuses on *how* the executive team integrates to address the content issues placed in front of it. Effective relationship dynamics, clear roles and responsibility definitions, authenticity, and clarification of how power is used are essential for creating a powerful and effective management team—a Top Team—from a group of skilled players.

Observing the effectiveness of its own internal

processes is a talent rarely seen within an executive team. It is not what its members get paid to do. Utilizing an external, unbiased resource that is conversant in your business, has a sensitive ear for how people are interrelating, and has garnered enough trust from the players creates a powerful ROI. It is possible to educate a group of diverse players—even technical, hard-nosed people—to willingly observe and comment on their own process of discussion and to distinguish dialogue from argument, defensiveness from openness, and progress from stasis.

4. The soft stuff drives the hard stuff: Alignment requires a balance of dynamics and team building (the soft stuff) as well as an unwavering focus on competitive strategy, clear deliverables, and effective implementation (the hard stuff). Executives often ask, "Why is the soft stuff so hard to do?" Simply put, because they have never been trained to focus on it.

   Any successful Advance will rely not on "feel-good sessions" but on hard, measurable results, with clear feedback for an effective increase in performance. Good Advances are results-driven, not "touchy-feely." Discussion of strategy will result in actionable steps for implementation. Increasing clarity about roles will result in better accountability. Feedback will result in measurable behavior change.

   It is less stressful, more productive, and individually more fulfilling to work with people you trust and, hopefully, like, but the bottom line is still about value, profit, customers, and the art of communication.

5. Don't try this at home: Using an experienced advisor, coach, or facilitator is a critical factor in success. Any

substantive Advance must deal with issues without censoring or editing differences of opinion. To ensure that these issues make it on the agenda and are dealt with openly and fully, using an unbiased and experienced outside resource is always the best choice. It is important to choose wisely. Well-meaning consultants without industry-specific knowledge will lack context and an understanding of your world. Industry experts will do a good job focusing on the content but cannot deal with the critical dynamics. Make sure the facilitator has the "ten thousand hours" of experience he or she needs to work with your team. Make sure this person does his or her homework. Interviews with team members and their reports, and a thorough understanding of the organization, including its history, current conditions, culture, and style, are essential for success.

6. If it ain't broke, who cares? Schedule Advances regularly. Building an aligned executive team requires work and frequent maintenance. The more regular the meetings, the easier they become. Time spent on strategy, on the proactive, front-end pieces, produces competitive advantage. Don't wait for something to break or for there to be pain in the system before convening an Advance. This diminishes the impact of the event, the return on your energy, and the credibility of the leader. Foresight is less painful than hindsight and is the shorter path to lucrative results.

7. Lastly, have some fun: While it is called "work" for a reason, a good team needs the lubricant of laughter and irreverence to want to work together and produce great results. Time spent in relationship and acknowledgment

of what you have accomplished together makes the good times better and the tough times shorter.

Interview as Intervention

We always begin the Advance process by interviewing all of the key stakeholders who will be in attendance and many of the key people who contribute to, depend on, or have critical intersections with the senior team. It is not uncommon for us to interview twenty or more people, including some administrative assistants (who always know what is going on). While the interviews are anonymous and what people say is nonattributable, we look for the important themes that emerge from the process. Those themes are what informs and builds the agenda.

> "When culture and change collide ... culture usually wins."

For many years we missed the obvious: the fact that the interview process itself is a form of intervention. Some things would seem to reoccur. We'd find out that Fred and Melissa had significant and longstanding issues of mistrust, that their communication was strained, and that this was creating difficulties in how their teams communicated and collaborated with one another. Certainly this would become an item for us to address and resolve in the Advance, or it would be a "moose" that everyone knew about and no one would bring up. Somehow, when the time for the Advance was approaching, we would hear that Melissa and

> "An Advance focuses on how the executive team integrates to address the content issues placed in front of it."

Fred had scheduled a series of ongoing lunch meetings together. They would let some people know that they had reached an understanding with each other. Was this simply great timing? Actually, it was the interview process acting as a catalyst and intervention.

We do these deep dives for other reasons as well. They introduce us to participants, who are often nervous about the upcoming Advance. They need to know that the person designing and facilitating the process is credible and will have the requisite chemistry, experience, and humor to do this

> "Why is the soft stuff so hard to do?"

well. Yet another reason is the aforementioned need to get the right issues on the table. As facilitators, we learn the business, get a sense of how the informal organization works, and begin to tee up the issues that must be addressed and resolved to take the team to a new level of awareness and performance. We also begin to expose those dynamics that exist just below the surface that shape everything the team does.

Dynamics, Dynamics, Dynamics

Dynamics are to teams as current is to water. While often not visible, they influence and touch everything that occurs. If you have ever had the experience of "swimming against the tide," either literally or within a corporate environment, you are fighting the dynamics that you can't see but do feel.

Much as psychotherapists work to move the unconscious and preconscious into awareness, our work with teams involves moving the unspoken into open dialogue. We surface the informal culture in such a way that people can make deliberate and conscious decisions about how to behave with one another. Much like culture, dynamics always exist even when they are not clearly visible or defined. Since teams are a form of systems, we pay attention to the various relationships, groups, cliques, informal networks, shared history, diversities, and similarities that serve to draw people together or separate them. We look at issues of power, turf, security, ambition, personality, and who is viewed as competent, hardworking, and trustworthy within the team. We get a good glimpse of what individuals value, which deeply influences their commitment to their jobs and sense of belonging to the group.

One thing we do deliberately is bring dynamics to the surface in a way that normalizes them. We work to remove the mystery of motivation, of avoidance, of less-than-full commitment in a nonthreatening, yet human and often humorous, way.

Several years ago a large pharmaceutical company asked me to coach one of its executives who was extraordinarily bright, very ambitious, and impatient. The company culture was "nice," and those who were both impatient and ambitious did not fit in and were suspect in their intentions. Jöerg (fictitious name), the executive, was resistant to having someone from the outside try to "shrink his head," but he consented to an interview in his office. He was about fifteen minutes late, so I sat in his office and observed. When he came in he asked, "So, what do you think you will learn about me sitting here that you couldn't have learned on the phone?" I replied, "You are really crazy about your kids—especially your younger girl. And you are very proud of your last team's achievements and publications." His face changed from impatient to confused. All I had done was look at his kids' drawings and the modest but visible award plaque from a pharmaceutical awards conference he had attended. I then asked, "How old were you when you decided to cure multiple sclerosis?"

He looked up in surprise as I pointed out that he had a picture of a man in a wheelchair partially hidden behind his computer. He said, "I was sixteen, and this reminds me of my promise to my dad every day." Was Jöerg ambitious? Yes, but not about his position in the company. Was he arrogant? Not really—he was demanding and pushed hard. But nobody around him knew what drove him, what his purpose was—what he was *for*. He was asked to head a new and important committee, and there were a lot of rumblings about him being at the helm. I suggested to him that he begin the meeting by asking the question, "Why is each of us really here?" He laughed, but when he saw this was a serious suggestion he consented to do it. I told him (a little white lie) that it was a good beginning for a new team and would not take too long. He called late the next day to tell me that the team took six hours to go through the exercise and that it was the most powerful thing he had ever done. This was the first time he had ever told his story to his peers. Over the next three years, he received two promotions and is now viewed as a hard-driving, focused guy who is transparent about who he is and what drives him.

A long story, to be sure, but an example of taking a hidden dynamic and making it more visible. Even when people are fearful that surfacing something will make the situation worse, our experience is just the opposite. With few exceptions in a long career, putting the moose on the table gives people an opportunity to surface what is important, to have guided dialogue about it, and to clear it as a dynamic that is not visible but very present.

This happens in a good Advance and forms a powerful basis for trust and a foundation for taking increased risks together as a Top Team.

Calling Audibles

It is virtually unthinkable to go into a multiday off-site Advance without an agenda that is carefully constructed in collaboration with the senior executive of the team. We have seen agendas that are so carefully constructed that breaks and specific discussions are orchestrated and carefully timed. This is done for good reason: time away from the office is valuable, and members of a team want to ensure that they are addressing those priorities that are relevant for the business in a setting and context that provides a different opportunity for dialogue. In fact, we almost always begin an Advance by asking what people want from the time together. We may ask what the "worst" results might be—those that would occur if the off-site failed or languished. We also ask for the "best" results—those that would indicate tremendous success and value for the time spent together. And we ask how this time together is (or should be) different from normal meetings or other off-sites. We have yet to hear anything other than compelling reasons for the team to come together now for the purpose of having open dialogue about real issues. And, no matter how good a team is, it always believes it can be better—that the bar can be raised even higher.

So we begin with an agenda that is built on interviews with team members or a working knowledge of those issues that the team needs to talk about now and next. While I have heard tales of facilitators who actually follow agendas from start to finish, that has rarely been my experience. I think of agendas as directional guidelines that set a series of expectations for the meeting, but my experience and bias is to follow the dialogue and the energy in the room. Following agendas will always cut off important dialogue in which the "next thing" won't be said. Conversely, not having an agenda can lead to multiple rabbit trails of unfocused and unfinished discussions. The art and science of a great meeting is "calling the audible": changing the agenda and direction to fit what is most important and thus where the dialogue must go.

Buckminster Fuller (1981) once said that having a goal is important but that real value enters *"at right angles."* What he meant was that having a goal is important, as it creates motion toward an outcome, but how you get to that outcome is by following the strands and scents of the dialogue in the room. In other words, if it is important, you pursue it. So calling audibles that continually rebuild the original agenda is the natural sign of a good Advance. One word of caution here: it's good to announce beforehand that these audibles will likely occur, as there are linear people in the world who will get nervous if they think progress, as measured by adherence to the agenda, is not being made.

Creating Rules of Engagement

In earlier chapters, we talked about the power of a collective future and the need to align the stars around that agreed-upon and compelling future state. We opined that there is not one "right" type of team, as the specific strategy and larger senior purpose will define the type of team you need to build. We talked about how important it is for teams to understand how they function under pressure and what their default setting is under stress. And we spent some time looking at the importance of understanding and managing paradox, as teams very frequently deal with both the Now and the New at the same time.

Top Teams, without fail, create rules of engagement— behavioral agreements about how members are going to operate together. Many years ago, as a young consultant with the Atlanta Consulting Group, I learned a very simple management axiom called "management by agreement," which has stood the test of time. Management by agreement has four simple parts:

1. Make only those agreements you intend to keep.

2. Do not make fuzzy agreements (anything that is unclear).

3. Ensure that what you do and what you say match up.

4. If you have to break an agreement, give notice, and if you break an agreement, apologize.

Management by agreement is based on the premise that if people give their word, they will do their best to keep it. Making agreements in the interest of the team and in the interest of creating and maintaining good dialogue (trust over peace) is important.

In the course of facilitating a good Advance, we create a set of operating ground rules (rules of the road/rules of engagement). These ground rules are simple, powerful behavioral agreements about how people will conduct themselves in the service of the meeting and of the team. While this is not rocket science or even a novel approach in meeting facilitation, creating ground rules is often done as kind of a throwaway, get-it-done exercise that loses the power of an agreement. But in the way we use ground rules, they are much more than an exercise or agenda item.

Before I give examples of ground rules, let's talk about trust, the supercharged word that comes up in every interview I have ever done with team members—usually the one issue that is most often avoided in meetings together. If we get into the definitional aspects of the word *trust*, it may mean not trusting that a person will do what he or she says. It may mean that you do not trust this person to represent your interests if you are not in the room. Or it may mean that this person does not have an operational track record or the competencies to do what he or she promises. It has other meanings as well, but the bedrock that underlies trust, and the only antidote I know to repairing broken trust is a conscious commitment to building high credibility—the making and keeping of agreements.

We use ground rules for two purposes: to set the behavioral stage for an Advance and to provide teams with a working example of making and keeping agreements that they can use as an operating template in the workplace. Agreement by a team on a series of ground rules/rules of engagement involves making the informal more formal, the unexpressed more articulated, and sometimes the obvious more explicit. But it is, at its heart, the foundation upon which team members will take the risk of putting themselves out there with one another and having important dialogue about things that matter. It is the bedrock on which individuals will confront one another and fight for something meaningful. And it becomes a form of internal contracting in which people give their word—and attempt to keep it.

There are some ground rules that are especially valuable. The list below is helpful yet far from exhaustive. And it is important to restate that ground rules should be constructed with the team, not simply be a series of words imposed by a consultant.

We will:

1. *operate with positive intentionality and wear an enterprise hat;*

2. *participate fully—say what we think even if it's not fully formed;*

3. *respect the opinions and ideas of others;*

4. *welcome contrarian points of view (speak our mind);*

5. *label how decisions get made and support decisions made by the group both publicly and privately;*

6. *take ownership for the success of this team and of this meeting;*

7. *respect agreements on time, attendance, and focus;*

8. *agree that what is said in the room stays in the room; and*

9. *act on what we agree to—and expect that others will as well.*

A couple of things are notable in this brief list. First is the active language of "We will." This involves asking people to give active agreement to the process. It does not work to simply ask the question, "Does everyone agree?" and get head nods. And it certainly is a bad idea to say, "If no one disagrees, we'll move forward." Remember—silence does not constitute agreement. You want an active and energetic "Yes!" as you ask whether the people in the room will fully and completely play by these rules. Making and keeping agreements are key.

One more thing to remember is that these rules, much like your strategy, are not cast in stone. It is good to periodically "renew your vows" and check in with the team about what each one of these agreement means to them, and add or edit as required.

As we do our after action review (AAR) of our off-site, we will usually review the ground rules, ask how they were helpful, what we need to edit or change, and whether the group wants to take them back into their day-to-day world. Having behavioral agreements "back home" makes a big and discernable difference in how people relate to one another and brings both increased civility and raised expectations for good dialogue in the business.

Questions

The Need for High-Order Dialogue

- Who is the dominant force behind your culture? What kind of culture does this create?

- What are the behaviors in your organization that lead to public agreement but private complaining? What is the cost to the organization?

- To what extent do people on your team feel able to shoot straight, differ publicly, raise different ideas, and dialogue fully?

- Do you rate the quality of your meetings? Do you occasionally stop in the middle of a meeting and ask how it can be improved? What would be the value in doing so?

- In your team, how candid are you with one another? Do you leave meetings with unaddressed and unresolved issues? What is the cost of doing so?

- What do you do to deliberately improve your ability as a team to truly engage issues and create effective dialogue?

- Does your CEO/leader trust you to tell the full truth?

Differentiating an Advance from a Retreat

- How often does your team have an Advance—a meeting designed to produce open and real dialogue about the most important issues?

- How often do you revisit your strategy and assess what is changing in your world?

- How often do you adjust your priorities?

- Can you, and do you, talk as a team about the issues that get in your way? Think about one or two issues that are unspoken but important to talk about. What would it take to do this inside your team? What would you gain if you did this well?

- How open, how candid, and how productive are you in your dialogue together? What could make this even better?

- Do you regularly do after action reviews (AARs)? How would you make the next meeting even better than this one?

INTERVIEW AS INTERVENTION

- How often do you have an experienced third party interview members of the team to assure that the important issues are making it to the table?

- Who is around that knows the team, the players, the business, the dynamics, the default settings, and how the team could be even better?

DYNAMICS, DYNAMICS, DYNAMICS

- How would you describe the dynamics within your team? What are the positive dynamics that make you as good as you are? What are the underlying dynamics that interfere with your being a Top Team?

- Do you have a process for surfacing and addressing the dynamics inherent within your team?

- Do the unsaid things get said? Are there "unmention-ables" around which people tread lightly?

- How would it improve your team performance if you were "clean"—in other words, if nothing important was left unsaid?

Calling Audibles

- Are your off-sites driven by and wedded to very specific agendas?

- How flexible are you, as a team, in calling audibles that change your direction when necessary?

- Can you give an example in which calling an audible changed your direction in a very positive and productive way?

Creating Rules of Engagement

- Do you have well-articulated behavioral agreements between team members?

- Do they apply back at the office?

- Are these agreements understood and utilized across the larger organization?

- Is this how the informal organization operates?

CHAPTER 7
Growing and Sustaining Top Teams

ROBERT CAMPBELL, MD, IS A *pediatric cardiologist and medical director of Sibley Heart Center at the Children's Hospital of Atlanta. He is a doctor, a businessman, and a good leader. He trained hard for the first, but has had to learn the other two. As a student of leadership, he has created physician and health-care leadership teams within his practice and across the hospital system that have made a significant difference in the care of patients, the economic well-being of his practice, and the morale of his physicians and their health-care teams. In a recent conversation, Robert told me that developing a sustainable leadership team within his large practice was one of the most unusual things he has ever done—and one of the most important. Physicians are trained to be individual contributors, yet work in teams with other health-care professionals to provide care—in this case to very sick children. How did Dr. Campbell build these teams and create a culture of leadership within Sibley?*

*They began, as do all Top Teams, with a clear statement about their purpose—what they are **for**. For Sibley Heart Center, the key word was "care." As Robert said, "We are in the caring business—providing care is what we do. Care is a noun, caring a verb, and being a caring professional a requirement." So for Sibley, care is not a vision statement, but rather a well-defined and agreed-upon way of being. This has become the uniting factor among this big group of pediatric cardiologists. And it didn't emerge from the marketing department. Rather, it was the result of open dialogue within the group about what mattered most, which in turn became the catalyst to a process of alignment and the creation of a structured leadership team behind this compelling core value.*

They didn't stop there. Leadership is a conscious and deliberate process. It is not automatic or instinctual. It is contextual—being a leader inside a complex healthcare environment has similarities to being a leader anywhere, yet the environment and context dictate who is involved, what success looks like, how it is measured, and what dialogue needs to address. Robert worked hard with his team, defining and assessing leadership competencies, bringing good consultants in to coach top people, exploring the historical and current team dynamics, and providing governance and solid structural advice. These busy doctors read leadership articles and attend conferences—and do so willingly. It has become important to them and to the system in which they work. And now the Top Team at Sibley Heart Center is comprised of "students of leadership"—people who are committed to becoming even better leaders than they currently are, and creating even better teams than they were (Campbell personal conversation).

Building Relational Intelligence (RI)

There is no shortage of writing on the concept and practice of emotional intelligence (EI), and the data is compelling. Most people in senior leadership positions do not lack raw intellectual horsepower, a strong work ethic, high integrity, and a deep knowledge of the business they are in or came from. What differentiates very successful senior leaders from those who are less successful is their ability and willingness to know themselves— their strengths and weaknesses, their default settings, their performance under stress, their hot buttons and conflict styles, and the kinds of people they feel at ease with or uncomfortable being around.

EI is a classic case of the "soft stuff driving the hard stuff." Leaders may get feedback from a variety of sources over their careers, such as 360 evaluations, leadership style assessments, assessment center results, and the like. In fact, most executive coaching is focused on improving key interpersonal skills, such as listening better, communicating more frequently, giving feedback to others, and becoming more transparent in intention. Becoming more emotionally intelligent is a prerequisite for being a member of a Top Team, as it is, at its very core, all about doing a better job of knowing yourself and taking that knowledge into your work with others.

When we talk about relational intelligence (RI), we are focusing on creating the process and chemistry for having dialogue— about almost anything. RI is about knowing how to connect with others—to listen in a way that is authentic, empathetic, and focused, and to communicate while staying in connection. This last point about connection to others is important, as what we refer to as communication is an essential, but highly general, term that covers a lot of ground.

Relational Intelligence (RI) and Top Teams

One of the observations we frequently hear is that not all teams are created equal. Building a Top Team always starts with the team you have. While that might sound obvious, think of the difference between a start-up team, a team that is tasked to "fix" a broken system, and an established, already highly performing team. Each has its unique dynamics and issues that have to be understood, addressed, and resolved.

In each case, there is one dynamic—that of trust—that is essential to building and sustaining the team. And it is in building and sustaining trust that RI is of critical importance.

Let's look at a team whose mission is to improve performance in a system or industry that has struggled with market share, operating issues, changes in leadership, or with team composition. In most cases, its emphasis is to "perform"—to get the operating and functional sides working well, make the numbers, and keep promises to the board. Building or fixing a business requires going "deep" into the issues and takes an enormous amount of time and focus from leaders. In the process, there is huge focus on dealing with the Now and the New as leaders/managers look to clarify roles, responsibilities, and decision rights within their business or function.

What often happens is that professional silos, or "sandboxes," are created in which people work deep but not wide, given their focus of improvement. While they navigate those matrices where essential functions intersect with operations, they must also collaborate across the horizontal chains of supply, delivery, and what it takes to go to market. What we often hear within the team are messages that sound like, "I'm too busy and too deep within my own function to help you fix yours." While this may be an overstatement for many teams that understand the need for collaboration, it is nonetheless true as a default setting. Creating these "blinkers" is understandable but, nonetheless, does nothing to improve collaboration, ideation, and trust within the team.

Relational Capital and Trust

In most cases, trust becomes a casualty of not taking the time to build good relationships. Nick Wall (personal conversation), VP of human resources for the Coca Cola Bottling Investment Group, one of the most diverse companies in the world, has a unique view of how global teams come together. His view is that building relationships is absolutely essential in knitting together teams of diverse professionals across cultures faced with challenging business issues. Nick states, *"The most critical piece in building teams is the time spent building relationships. This becomes the baseline of our trust and liking for one another and the best way to bridge cultural obstacles."* His observation is that the relational/personal interaction between team members, largely honed through deliberate, informal time together, is one of the most important things in building great teams. It also becomes the accelerant that allows new people to join teams (which is a foundation for driving collective intelligence [CI]).

RI requires a basis of good EI—a strong knowledge of one's own strengths, derailers, and default settings. EI is essential in building relationships and trust with another. And trust is built on the bedrock of credibility—of making and keeping agreements, of listening and understanding what another person is *for*, and

> "In many cases, trust becomes a casualty of not taking the time to build good relationships."

doing all that you can to support that. In many cases, RI is a function of time spent with others—over coffee, dinner, or adult beverages, and with families. But to accelerate the process when time is of the essence and new people are involved, you need to create those moments of dialogue through regular Advances, as we mentioned earlier.

Good RI is a conscious and deliberate process that serves to build the aforementioned trust and collaboration—critical components of Top Teams. As Mickey Connolly (personal conversation) of Conversant states, "It is important that people stay more connected to what they are *for* than what they are *against*."

How often have you had the experience of feeling truly connected to another person, whether at ease or highly challenged, when you were willing to openly communicate your opinions and thoughts? This is often referred to as the "willingness to say the next thing," as our normal censors and edits tend to govern what is appropriate, risky, or politically correct. But it is in the presence of another—who asks good questions, who listens, who challenges, who responds authentically, and who furthers the conversation—that we feel most connected, and at our best with another human being.

Experienced teams in stable businesses have an advantage in that people generally know one another better. Since relationships are more established, predictability and trust tend to be higher. But this can have its own unique downside if the thinking of the group gets rusty or too comfortable. Strong or successfully evolving businesses with high-performing teams tend to have a better balance of the Now and the New in that they have effectively decoded and continue to drive execution excellence down through their companies while utilizing the senior team to think strategically and collectively.

It's Always about Communication

Communication occurs in many ways. For instance, leaders should be able to talk to groups of employees, to hold all-hands meetings, to brief a board of directors or their own CEO, or to stand in front of customers and hear their feedback. This is part of requisite communication and is a form of RI. As my good friend Bill MacKinnon (personal conversation)—expert teacher of communication and presentation—said to us, "It is critical to establish communication at the moment that portends a relationship to come." Bill is referring to communication that is stimulating, motivating, and energetic—in which the "self" is activated in the listener. With high RI, others experience you as authentic, transparent, and caring about them.

Mickey Connolly, co-author of *The Communication Catalyst*, and a former hostage negotiator and restaurateur, describes communication as a deliberate and conscious practice that takes place at what he identifies as "the intersection of you, the other person, and the context in which it occurs" (Connolly and Reardon 2002). Mickey sees communication, at its finest, as creating "high-velocity value," which requires that we elicit or create a deep understanding of the point of view of someone whose support we desire and discover where our interests overlap with theirs. While this is referred to as "bridging" in influence models, it carries with it some nonnegotiable actions:

1. Understanding and respecting the important *purpose* of the other person—what they are *for*

2. Understanding the concerns they have about not achieving their purpose

3. Understanding the circumstances or obstacles that affect their purpose

If you cannot understand and acknowledge all three of the above nonnegotiable actions in someone else, your voice and opinion will not be heard. Your admission ticket to the conversation rests on your ability to elicit the above and listen deeply—what Mickey calls, "Listening for the essential purpose."

RI differs from its first cousin EI in that it puts more emphasis on how committed and effective we are in connecting to other people. For those of us who have spent the time required getting to know ourselves—our unique "style"—and developing our EI (always an ongoing journey), we have to be equally diligent and committed to developing our RI. One of my dubious distinctions in graduate school was writing the first published doctoral dissertation using the Myers-Briggs Type Indicator. After having the usual postgraduate experience of not looking at what I had written (or learned) for eight years, I attended an MBTI course at the Center for Applications of Psychological Type in Gainesville, Florida (Go Gators). I was very impressed with the center's practical view of how our stylistic and often hardwired differences play out in the real world and in our relationships with others. Given our differences, whether they are about extraversion or introversion or other styles, we, as leaders and members of Top Teams, must have a common commitment to building our RI, as that is the bridge between us and another.

Top Teams need to have the requisite dialogue that enables them to challenge every assumption; to think broadly, deeply, and laterally; and to harness the CI of their group. And this requires a very deliberate and conscious practice of RI.

If we flash back to the opening example in this chapter of Dr. Campbell and the Sibley Team, these physicians have had to learn things they weren't taught in medical school about how they must keep improving themselves individually as leaders and collectively as a team.

Zooming in and Zooming Out

We have talked about the need for Top Teams to address the Now and the New—the essential current realities and the external and emerging environment. How Top Teams balance their time and utilize their expertise in both spheres requires holding both the Now and the New simultaneously as a paradox that must be managed, not a problem to be solved. By the same token, Top Teams also must have the capability to *zoom in*—to get to the devils in the details, the numbers, and the tactics—and to *zoom out*—to see the larger picture from the contextual, systemic, and market-oriented view.

This is not easy. One brief simulation we often do with teams is to give each member a picture that, if put together sequentially, tells a story. It may begin with a view of Earth from space and through numerous iterations shows a picture of Earth in a storybook, in a home, in a village, near the ocean, under the sky, looking up at the stars. We ask people to find others who have pictures similar to theirs and eventually tell the story together. It is a simple exercise that few teams do well given their makeup, their default settings, and sometimes how ambiguous we are with instructions. But it is an illustrative exercise that demonstrates that most team members have a preferred style, usually reinforced by their work experience, which leads them to favor zooming in on the details or zooming out to the bigger picture. The point is—Top Teams need to do both.

One of the standard ways of thinking about team development is that teams that are made up of people who are similar—the classic example of an old boys' network in which leaders choose members who are much like themselves—form more quickly and have less conflict. They share and value similar styles. The downside is that they also share common blind spots. Teams that are more diverse in style typically take longer to form and work out their differences but have fewer blind spots, as they have greater coverage from tactical to strategic, from detail orientation to big picture, and from numbers to market needs. Given your experience on teams, what is your thinking about forming a team and deciding, as Jim Collins is often quoted, "Who is on the bus?" (Collins 2001)

One of the major premises of this book is that you build the team you need to actualize your strategy. This may mean that as the world around you changes, so does your strategy and so may your team. But in reality, Top Teams that have been together for a while have demonstrated, at their core, that they have the agility, CI, and diversity of thinking, held together by a common purpose, to enable them to respond well to changes in the market, to adapt to changes in technologies, and to take on the challenges before them. This is rarely automatic and much more frequently represents deliberate thinking about the needs and makeup of the team. The obvious example is the CEO who is big-picture and macro-focused who selects people that bring more detailed and operationally focused preferences to the table. Not a bad strategy on the surface.

But as you go deeper and look at the capabilities of the team, you may find the CEO (and maybe the "strategy guy") as the self-designated outward-looking outlier and the rest of the team, both functional and operational, as the detail-oriented folks. So the CEO demonstrates good EI by knowing his or her strengths and weaknesses and thus compensates by hiring people who are stylistically different. Is this a good idea? Let's look further.

What happens when the task-oriented team comes together for a meeting? How much dialogue is there among team members? How do they utilize their CI? Do the operationally and financially focused leaders contribute to the larger strategic discussion? What kind of teams do they, in turn, build that have the requisite diversity of style and capabilities to zoom in and out? How do they develop people who are not like them in the service of the larger enterprise? Building a Top Team that has real diversity—in thinking style, in experience, in culture, in the ability to zoom in and zoom out—is both a conscious choice and a constant practice.

Collaborate to Calibrate: Building Teams One to Three Levels Down

I recently attended a talent management review designed to identify and fast-track high-potentials and future leaders of this firm. The team members had done their homework. Individual assessments, previous work histories and evaluations, and recent photographs were presented. Future leaders were rated with the classic nine-box method and, with little surprise, most were within the upper-right quadrant. Then Rick, the president of the division chimed in and asked, "How are we calibrating success?" There was a pause in the conversation. People were used to this exercise as is, not with questions. Rick asked again, "We know who these folks are and what they have done, but what capabilities do we need going forward? What kind of leaders do we need? What characteristics must they have?" Thus began a four-hour dialogue among the team members. The challenge before them was to collaborate on calibrating the leadership that would be needed going forward. It was a great discussion and a terrific team-building experience as they looked at history and to the future, at the Now and the New, at the ability for future leaders to zoom in and out, at their strengths and what they had yet to learn.

The human resources and talent development communities

usually take the point on the identification and development of emerging leaders, but theirs is a tough job. They have access to the senior team only once or twice a year, during which they present candidates and have a time-structured discussion about each potential leader. In a more ideal, but not unrealistic, world, senior leaders decide what they are looking for Now in terms of performance from candidates, and articulate, as best they can, what capabilities they are looking for in the New. Can they know exactly? Probably not. But they can create the experiences, exposure, mentoring, coaching, and contact to engage the next generations in the emerging future of their organization.

Marshall Goldsmith, one of our dear friends and renowned leadership expert, makes the point that there should be no surprises during a performance review, as there are six coaching questions that should always be in play between any leader and her/his reports:

1. Where are we going? The executive outlines where the larger organization is going in terms of vision, goals, and priorities. The executive then asks the direct reports where they think the larger organization should be going.

2. Where are you going? Direct reports discuss where their part of the organization should be going. By the end of this discussion two types of alignment should have been achieved: (a) the vision, goals, and priorities of the direct reports' parts of the organization should be aligned with the executives' vision of the larger organization, and (b) the individual goals and priorities of executives and direct reports should be aligned.

3. What is going well? Executives begin this part of the dialogue with an assessment of what the direct reports and their organizations are doing well. Then executives

ask their direct reports a question that is seldom asked, "What do you think that you and your part of the organization are doing well?

4. What are key suggestions for improvement? Executives give direct reports constructive suggestions for the future. These suggestions should be limited to key "opportunities for improvement." Next, executives should ask another (seldom-asked) great coaching question, "If you were your own coach, what suggestions would you have for yourself?"

5. How can I help? One of the greatest coaching questions an executive can ask is, "How can I help?" Executives can begin by listening to their direct reports' suggestions on how they can become more helpful.

6. What suggestions do you have for me? Leaders who ask for suggestions from their direct reports, focus on improving one or two key behaviors, and follow up on a quarterly basis, are almost always seen as dramatically increasing in leadership effectiveness.

This is personal dialogue at its finest—and it takes surprisingly little time to have this conversation every quarter or so. The result is that there are no surprises; there is high engagement of staff and a much higher probability that the leader will know the capabilities and needs of the next level of mission-critical people.

> "If you were your own coach, what suggestions would you have for yourself?'

Without question, one of the most important responsibilities of the senior team is to develop the next generation of leaders. But how good is their thinking about developing the next generation of teams? Does the senior team spend the time and resources and possible investment to build team capabilities one to three levels down the organization? Are future leaders exposed to the organization's strategic worldview and to emerging trends and technologies? Do they have a point of view about leadership that compels them to look both inside and relationally, at EI and RI? No doubt they have to perform well and execute flawlessly, but how are they trained to be more deliberate, conscious, and disciplined members of Top Teams?

If we simplistically take the view that teams one to three levels down from the top have mostly operational or functional responsibilities, that their role is to deal with pre-ordained targets, and that their fundamental responsibility is to execute in the Now, then the Top Team has a responsibility to provide them with the best tools available to create execution excellence. The Top Team also needs to provide them with a conscious and deliberate approach to create great teamwork and collaboration within their area and across the organization. In other words – to become a Top Team themselves. This is dialogue about investment that does not occur frequently or deeply enough within senior teams, which have the ultimate responsibility for setting the direction of the company and investing in future leadership in both the Now (execution excellence) and the New (strategic thinking).

Questions

BUILDING RELATIONAL INTELLIGENCE (RI)

- How have you used EI to build increased self-awareness as a leader?

- How have you used data from 360s, style assessments, conflict inventories, etc., to develop your leadership effectiveness?

- Has this been sustainable? Does it retain value over time for you?

- How would you define RI?

Relational Intelligence (RI) and Top Teams

- How deliberate and conscious are you and members of your team in creating RI to improve collaboration, ideation, and trust within your team?

- To what extent do you spend time together informally to build RI and get to know one another?

Relational Capital and Trust

- How willing are you to "say the next thing," to challenge your peers, to ask for support, to trust their intention toward you?

- How do you link RI, trust, collaboration, and effectiveness together?

- What would increased trust look like in your team?

- How deliberate is your practice of building RI within your team and across your network?

It's Always about Communication

- How well do members of your team communicate—really communicate—with one another?

- Do people on your team know what you are really *for*? Do you know what they are *for*?

- Do you understand the obstacles they

"What would increased trust look like in your team?"

have to achieving their purpose? Do others know your obstacles?

- What would it be like if communication was even better than it is?

Zooming in and Zooming out

- How well does your team zoom in (get into the details, numbers, and tactics)?

- How well does it zoom out (see the larger picture, context, and systemic view)?

- What is the default setting of the team?

- Do you have the capabilities to do both well?

- What could you do even better? What would be the payoff?

Collaborate to Calibrate:
Building Teams One to Three Levels Down

- How well do you talk about talent against the leadership needs of the company?

- Do you look at high performers' EI, RI, and CI in addition to their track records of performance?

- How well do executives "coach" their subordinates, high potentials, and one another in the service of building the team(s) and achieving the strategy?

- How deliberate are you in engaging and building teams one to three levels below you?

- How could you and your organization be better leadership developers, coaches, and mentors? What is the payoff?

CHAPTER 8

Being "That" Person: Great Teams Need Great Leaders

THIS BOOK BEGAN WITH A story about David, the general manager of an already successful division inside a large manufacturing company. David was committed to changing the culture of a long-standing, command-and-control organization into an organization of Top Teams that could drive growth, demonstrate the agility to capitalize on external challenges and internal changes, and execute flawlessly against their promises to the corporation and stockholders. David began his tenure as head of this division as he began everything else in his life—as one of the smartest people in the room. A sizable guy, he was quick to assess other people and make go-or-stay decisions about them, and he had a plan for growth and profitability already in mind. The issue was this: Could David become the kind of leader that could grow team and team member capability, that could foster the open and trusting dialogue needed to work across a large organization and between functions, that could build relational and collective intelligence (RI and CI), and that could grow teams one to three levels down? He had IQ points in abundance, but could he demonstrate the self-knowledge and relational abilities to pull this off given his intense style and personal default settings?

David engaged me as a coach and began the discussion (as many experienced leaders do) by telling me about his skepticism for the process and where the bodies of his former coaches were buried. We came to a strong understanding of what he was really **for**—growing as a leader and building his team and organization into a sustainable growth engine that the corporation wanted but whose culture often unintentionally prevented.

We spent the first several sessions getting to know one another—our histories, our real values (as told in stories), and what he most wanted in himself and from others. Any "coach" that was not fully committed to this journey with him would be destined to fail. He had to trust me and know I was experienced enough, tough enough, and had enough business savvy to stay in the ring with him. He also had to see that I was irreverent, mischievous, and humorous enough for us to spend the requisite time together building relational capital and trust. He had to know that I was committed to his success and to that of the organization.

It has been (and continues to be) a great journey for both of us. He is as committed to developing his own leadership and that of those around him as anyone I've ever met. His contribution to his division and to the culture of engagement he has created is remarkable. It's not easy, but it's fun to do this work. However, you have to know the territory.

The Person of the Leader:
Being Conscious and Deliberate

This book is about how to raise the bar of already good teams into what we have described as Top Teams—teams that succeed and thrive even as the world around them becomes more complex. While it would seem logical that great teams be comprised of great leaders, this is not always the case. In fact, it would be more accurate to say that great teams are made up of people who are committed to being even better leaders—people who are conscious and deliberate about their own learning and effectiveness as leaders and equally committed to growing their understanding of how teams continue to grow and develop.

As we said earlier, there is no one right type of team—the structure, makeup, and focus depend on what the strategy requires. It is equally true that there is no one right type of leader within a team. Leaders come in all sizes, shapes, and styles—from extraverted to introverted, from warm and caring to businesslike, from participative to command-and-control. What is true about good leaders who build and comprise great teams is that they are very conscious and deliberate about their leadership style and about what the team must continue to do. If they were to have an autopilot setting, it would be in the "off" position much of the time.

> "Great teams are made up of people who are committed to being even better leaders."

While there are many books on leadership, one of the most relevant and powerful leadership models can be found in Peter Koestenbaum's book *Leadership: The Inner Side of Greatness* (Koestenbaum 1991). Peter's diamond model of "leadership greatness" has four dimensions: vision, courage, reality, and ethics.

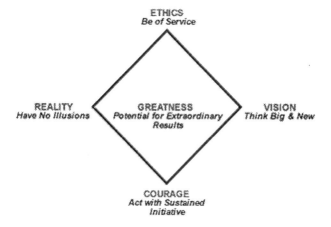

ETHICS
Be of Service

REALITY
Have No Illusions

GREATNESS
Potential for Extraordinary
Results

VISION
Think Big & New

COURAGE
Act with Sustained
Initiative

Koestenbaum makes the point that operating with a "leadership mind" involves a working balance between all four poles of the diamond, and that if any of the four dimensions is absent or minimized, people will operate in a less-than-great manner. For example, a leader who is visionary, has a great grasp of current reality, and is highly ethical, but who lacks courage, will have great ideas, but will not take the necessary risks to move forward. Leaders who have great ideas and are ethical and courageous can make terrible decisions if they don't have good facts and a grasp of current reality.

If we extrapolate from this model and look at how Top Teams operate, we must be aware of and work to ensure that all the points of the leadership compass are incorporated into teams' dialogue and decision-making. This is why teams are more capable of making better decisions than are individual leaders. If they have the right people on the bus and talk with each other about the right stuff, they will go forward with fewer blind spots and with collective courage.

There is so much written about leadership that echoes a consistent message. Yet there is less written about how teams can and should operate, and what they must do during chaotic and changeable times. As we stated earlier in this book, the world is changing mightily, and what we understand about change continues to evolve. That said, there are some common elements that apply to leaders within Top Teams—those teams that continue to raise the bar of performance both of the Now and the New.

Such leaders:

- Have high integrity, clear values, and a transparent way of operating. People around them know what to expect.

- Are committed to continual learning and development, individually and collectively.

- Are always looking outward and inward to the New. They have an eye to macroeconomics, technology, politics, customer needs, and the global situation.

- Understand their business and have a clear plan for the *Now*—their critical priorities and expectations for those who report to them. They know how to execute.

- Continue to deepen their knowledge of themselves (their EI) and their capacities to relate, listen, and influence others' RI.

- Work hard at communicating with their peers.

- Strive for balance and happiness as human beings (yes, even CEOs).

Rarely do good teams become great teams by accident. There is purposefulness about their evolution and a definite series of practices they follow. Think about any teams that have a moderate to high degree of interdependence—from sports teams to elite military teams. In most cases, they begin with people who are

highly qualified and have earned their
stripes by being serially successful
at the fundamentals of their job. In
their track record of success, they have
learned to play well with others—to
blend support of others with a tough-

> "Rarely do good teams become great teams by accident."

minded, edgy, playing-flat-out approach to the outside world.
They push each other and demand only the best. They almost
always have a coach—either someone who has been there before
and/or sees a future state and the road map to get there. Again,
this is true in sports, the military, medicine, and business. There
is someone or something that pushes the group to look deeper
and achieve more than they could have done by themselves.
And, these teams practice hard—through multiple scenarios that
qualify them for the next New experience. There is a saying that
"luck favors the prepared" and Top Teams follow that adage.
Military teams rehearse scenarios day after day. Great sports
teams rehearse everything from their opening set of plays to the
last-two-minute drills. Performers rehearse and rehearse.

So it is with Top Teams, who do two key things differently
from regular leadership teams.

First, they periodically step back from the day-to-day regular
or reactive operating rhythm to go through a series of "what if"
questioning. It reads like this, "Okay, folks, sales have been on
the uptick, and our operations seem to be in good shape, but
a conflict in Africa is driving the price of lead and copper up
dramatically. How can that impact us, and what do we do?" This
is a real simulation and a rehearsal of a potential New scenario.
Another potential scenario might be, "We have become a much
more global company by doing a great job of integrating our
manufacturing and supply chain with our South American
counterparts. A rapidly spreading global pandemic of type 3 bird

flu has begun in Mexico. There is talk of shutting down factories and even closing or restricting the border. We have two to three days before it impacts us. What do we do?"

These "what if" scenarios become practice situations in which teams recognize their interdependencies and deep abilities to communicate. But simulations never happen unless teams take the time to rehearse—to step back and think about this scenario practice.

"What if" your team spent time quarterly, perhaps as part of a regularly scheduled off-site Advance, to ask "what if" questions? We stated earlier that each Advance should begin with the question, "What is new or has changed in the world that could affect our business?" What if you followed that with scenario practice that ranged from potentially real issues that are just over the horizon, to some "crazier" scenarios that gave the team room to think more laterally together? Edward DeBono (1982), in his very interesting book *DeBono's Thinking Course*, gives a number of great examples of how a team can not only think together, but also *think about how they think together.* For example, if you were to ask the question, "What if all cars were yellow?" and record the answers, the answers would likely follow a predictable pattern based on bias toward color, and intelligence would be used to support the particular prejudice. You might then ask people to list the positive aspects of all cars being yellow, the negative aspects of all yellow cars, and then ask the question, "If all cars were yellow, it would be interesting to see ...." Now intelligence gets used to explore the subject more laterally. This is true for most subjects that come before a team. Experience often dictates immediate reaction. But Top Teams step back and think about how they approach a subject—what is the default response versus the "what if" response?

The work I do is great fun. I get to ask lots of interesting questions. I recently worked with a team of scientists who prided themselves on their ability to solve problems together. The afternoon of the second day, as part of their off-site time, they were planning to attend an Atlanta Braves baseball game. I asked them to come prepared the next morning to discuss all the ways the game would change if third base was removed. As predicted, it led to an interesting and fun discussion. But what was most enlightening to them was observing how they thought together. "What if" scenarios create a practice of exploring blind spots and appreciating the diversity of thinking in a good team.

A second key action that is a common practice of Top Teams is what is referred to as an after action review (AAR). This is a brutally honest dialogue that occurs shortly after an event as both a debrief and an immediate learning. It is group feedback, self-directed, and *always done* as part of how a Top Team operates. An AAR is comprised of four main questions:

1. What did we set out to do? (If the objectives were clear to begin with, this should be easy to answer.)

2. What actually happened? (The good, the bad, and the unexpected.)

3. Why did this happen?

4. What did we learn? (What would we repeat, do more or less of, or what do we need to study?)

This is a different experience from going from one event or crisis to another without taking the time to study, learn, and improve (or plan, do, study, and act, in quality language).

About ten years ago, I was asked to facilitate a series of meetings within a diverse team tasked with building what was, at that time, the largest cement plant in the world. This team was international in composition and made up of leaders from six different companies, all of which contributed critical expertise to the construction, outfitting, and certification of this large plant. As with any complex construction project, there were tremendous variables that created tremendous risk for a project that, if not finished on time, could cost up to $1 million a day in lost production and liquidated damages.

The steel for the project was being fabricated in Mexico, and delays in delivery kept mounting, thus throwing off the schedule despite heroic work-arounds by the contractor. At last we found ourselves in a windowless room, seven of us around a small table. The anxiety was palpable. The head contractor said, "Guys, I am doing everything that can be done here." And he meant it. A big guy from Belgium who was an equipment supplier banged his hand on the table and said, with great intensity, "No, dammit— you are not!" The contractor looked puzzled until the Belgian said, "You have not asked how we can help you." Six guys—all from different firms and countries—began to chip in. "I know someone in Colombia who has connections in the steel industry. Perhaps I can get him to the plant in Mexico." Another person said, "We do so much business in Mexico that we can expedite the permitting and transport of the steel." A third person volunteered extra trucks that could be moved from a project in Colorado. And so it went.

The story ended with the project slightly behind schedule— and that from a hurricane that no one could control. This was a group that recognized their interdependence at the last moment, and it was the diversity of their experience in global business and their willingness to use it together that saved them and the project. In retrospect, we should have done a better job of rehearsing potentially negative scenarios on the front end, yet the AAR was interesting as participants took their learning back to their parent companies and integrated these lessons into their day-to-day practices. I never forgot the lesson. Good teammates ask how they can help; they do not wait to be invited.

Coaching in Context

Over the past twenty years, the Levin Group has coached a lot of people across a wide range of industries. When we began, we tended to work with existing or promising executives, or those who were in trouble. One of the things we quickly learned is that *unless* you understand the unique business the executives are in, with the specific demands, intellectual requirements, structure, strategic direction, organizational and cultural history, key players, and more, your effectiveness as an influencer of behavior and as an advisor is limited. Our clients were always the first ones to know that. So our strong belief, shaped by many years of doing this, is that good coaching always occurs in the context of a specific business, and in that unique milieu; that is the team where the executive sits. You have to know the territory.

> "Good teammates ask how they can help. They do not wait to be invited."

We typically define good executive coaching as a strong relationship between a mission-critical leader and an experienced business consultant that is designed to accelerate the leader's and his or her team's effectiveness in achieving strategic, business, and interpersonal outcomes. Note that we define coaching to include "raising the bar of the team." And the understanding of context goes further. Understanding what a leader needs Now or Next requires that the coach be able to ask and understand the relevant strategic questions about the future vision for the organization and what it will require to create the requisite alignment. If the executive is being asked to be a growth leader, it may require that the coach understand the dynamics and demands of organic versus acquisitional growth. If the leader is addressing transitional challenges, such as how to operate successfully in a new role, it requires understanding both the demands and context of the new role as well as understanding the capabilities, strengths, and weaknesses that the leader brings from her or his old one. Coaching should always serve to increase interpersonal awareness and EI for leaders who don't realize their full impact upon others. Yet it can and should do even more, including address issues of decision-making, risk-taking, and building organizational courage and, ultimately, greater success.

Experience Matters—Ten Thousand Hours

Coaching is becoming a commodity, and while still valuable, it is beginning to lose the power and impact of its ability to, as Marshall Goldsmith says, "Help successful people get even better." Working at the top of the house is a different experience from simply debriefing a 360 and creating a development plan with little follow-up. Good coaching brings an intellectual and emotional challenge to the executive and requires an understanding of what is important to this person given the context, milieu, and challenges that he or she faces. Good intentions simply don't cut it.

In Malcolm Gladwell's fascinating book *Outliers*, he explores some of the unique characteristics that make people exceptional— even outstanding—in their field. Outside of some innate ability, his research indicates that there is a minimum level of practice that is the foundation for excellence. As Gladwell (2008) notes, "The idea that excellence at performing a complex task requires a critical minimum level of practice surfaces again and again in studies of expertise. In fact, researchers have settled on what they believe is the magic number for true expertise: ten thousand hours."

Ten thousand hours to be expert as a musician, a mathematician, a surgeon, or an executive coach. As we think of what is required to assist an experienced leader, who already has a track record of success, to raise the bar even higher, our experience tells us that executives want someone who can understand their business, understand them, and be someone they can talk to. This requires an experienced coach with the ten thousand plus hours of doing this work across multiple industries for many years. Developing leaders who create and sustain Top Teams is too important an investment to not do it right.

It's Lonely at the Top

This is more than an adage. Without fail, I ask leaders who they talk to about the pressures they face in navigating the Now and the New. It is rare that leaders say, "I talk to my team," or "I talk with my partners." More often than not, the response is that the higher people rise in an organization, the fewer people they can confide in. And, conversely, fewer people confide in them. This creates an experience of isolation that can be limiting for the leader and damaging for the organization. There is example after example of leaders not being fully in touch with what was happening within their own organization and multiple examples of teams that, because they didn't really talk to one another about the stuff that mattered, quietly conspired to damage or destroy their company.

I began this book by stating that creating and sustaining Top Teams is largely a dialogue process in which team members fully and completely talk about the stuff that matters. There is a Rule of One—that it only takes one person who knows something important and doesn't get the full attention of his or her peers or partners to destroy a business, a space shuttle, or the credibility of leadership. So who do the people at the top talk to?

The obvious answer should be that they talk openly and honestly to each other. This dialogue builds trust, as the leaders must be able to address anything and everything with one another. Yet, as we said earlier, this doesn't always come easily or naturally, even for the best leaders.

This is where a skilled facilitator/coach/consultant/trusted advisor can come into play. It is the facilitator or coach's job—his or her mission—to ensure that everything important is on the table and gets honestly addressed. It is a good facilitator's responsibility to know each of the people around the table—their histories, strengths, styles, default settings, derailers, and issues—and work with them to ensure that they are fully present and contributory with their team members. Rule of thumb: Nothing important goes unsaid. It is the responsibility of a skilled facilitator to understand the dynamics of power, personality, rank, and individual histories to facilitate dialogue that matters, and all this in the context of understanding the direction of the business and the challenges it faces.

So, to whom do leaders talk? They talk to a good coach or trusted advisor, for one, and, hopefully, they talk to their team. They begin with their trusted partners and expand the circle by creating a time, cadence, and process for them to talk as a larger team. Good facilitators who know their teams and have the experience to make this happen can make a difference. And, yes, experience does matter.

"You Can't Learn Less"—Leadership Development that Works

We hear about sustainability every day as it relates to how we use and value our most cherished resources. For leaders, time is one of the most valuable resources. So the practice of developing leaders and creating Top Teams must be accomplished in such a way as to add value that is both relevant and sustainable—it has to make a difference, and it has to last.

There has been no shortage of leadership or management training courses offered to organizations, especially to larger ones. In fact, I very often have the experience of being in an executive's office and asking about a 360 or a team evaluation or inquiring about how they have gone about development to see them rummage around the "credenza ware" to pull out old training manuals. "It's in here somewhere," refers to both the three-ring binders and their experience. The very best leadership and team development does several things:

1. it posits concepts and learning that are relevant and challenging for experienced leaders;

2. it uses real-world examples, so leaders can immediately apply learning to their tough challenges;

3. it brings people together to work and think as a team (and review how they worked and thought); and

4. it has sustainability to it—learning is "baked in" to team practice and culture.

Dave Myers (personal conversation) of Johnson Controls calls working on real-world examples "using live ammo," which we do in action learning, team simulations, and knowledge capture using the after action reviews (AARs) that we referenced earlier in this chapter.

For learning to be sustainable—and thus valuable to time-constrained leaders (even more problematic when you try to get an entire team together)—it has to become part of the culture of

> "The key to building credibility is to make only those agreements that you intend to keep (no matter what)."

the business. Culture is not just what Top Teams envision or the policies that are made to support this vision; it is also how the informal organization operates—in this case, how a team operates day to day. So, capturing key learnings from off-sites or training courses and then *agreeing* to use them in the real world are crucial to sustainability, value, and cultural change. Remember—no fuzzy agreements. The key to building credibility is to only make those agreements that you intend to keep (no matter what).

Sustainability: The Human Side

There is a human element to sustainability as well. CEOs and many senior team members operate as if they were an endangered species, and at the time of writing this book, they are. The CEO turnover rate doubled in 2005 and has continued to increase since then: more CEOs left their jobs in 2008 and 2009 than ever before in history (Wheeler 2010). Executive transition is a real issue and a very expensive proposition for companies.

Executives are stressed beyond comprehension. We have already talked about a world of increased complexity, volatility, ambiguity, and rate of change. We opined that executives struggle with isolation. Leaders within Top Teams have a responsibility to personally support one another—to be straightforward and demanding with clear expectations, but also to be aware of the humanity and personal sacrifice entailed in such leadership.

> "Sustainability is the increased capacity for people to survive and maintain the energy, health, and commitment to fully contribute to their life and livelihood."

About five years ago I interviewed the head of a division of a large manufacturing firm who had extraordinary energy and commitment for his job. He "proudly" announced that he had not been home for dinner in three years. I later asked members of his team why they allowed this if they wanted to keep him there and fully functional. My point was that they let him down in not challenging this behavior (which he was also modeling to his team). I've met a number of CEOs who live for the firm—but they don't seem to live long or especially well. One favorite of mine cruised the parking lot on Saturdays to see who was working. I put a sign on his desk that said, "If you are not here on Saturday don't bother coming in on Sunday!" It irritated him, yet got his attention. That was my job. The opposite of this example is a great and committed physician whose sister was ill. Her partners basically threw her out of the hospital door, insisting that she take the requisite time with her family and that they would cover for her. She was surprised and grateful for their generosity and caring, and when she returned, she was appreciative, committed, and renewed.

Sustainability is the increased capacity for people to survive and maintain the energy, health, and commitment to fully contribute to their lives and livelihoods. Top Teams are aware of this and provide the requisite support and challenge, sometimes using tough love, to help each other.

Questions

The Person of the Leader: Being Conscious and Deliberate

- How diverse is your team in terms of style, experience, and ways of thinking?

- To what extent are you, as a team, committed to continuing your individual and collective development as leaders and as a team?

- How do you ensure this occurs, given your time constraints?

- How often do you schedule "special time" off-site to explore issues, confirm your operating assumptions, and improve your level of play together?

- How often do you spend time rehearsing scenarios and deliberately thinking together?

- When was the last time you thought about how you think together?

- How often and how thoroughly do you do after action reviews (AARs)?

- Are these debriefs, postmortems, or explorations into what you learned and what you might do differently?

- Do you directly and frequently ask your teammates the question, "How can I help you?"

Coaching in Context

- How does your company utilize coaching?

- In your opinion, how well does it work?

- What has been your experience?

- What could your company do to improve the process to make it even better?

Experience Matters—Ten Thousand Hours

- Do you believe that the deep experience of a coach (ten thousand hours) really matters?

- How do you assess a coach's experience and background?

- How important is it for a coach to have a strong background in understanding personality style and interpersonal dynamics?

- Does a coach need to have an understanding of the business and the system that a person works within to be fully effective?

It's Lonely at the Top

- Who do you talk to?

- Can you discuss virtually anything ("put the moose on the table") with your team?

- Do you have a close-in and trusted advisor who knows your team and your business?

"You Can't Learn Less"—
Leadership Development that Works

- How sustainable and lasting has your experience with leadership training been?

- What experiences have been most valuable for you personally and for your team?

- In terms of leadership development and training, what works and what doesn't?

Sustainability: The Human Side

- Do you generally know what is going on with other members of your team? Do you express interest and genuinely care about how they are doing?

- Do you talk to one another about the pressures of the job?

CHAPTER 9

The Power of Integration

MY YOUNGER DAUGHTER AND I had dinner together one night at our favorite restaurant. She was seventeen, a senior in high school, and was taking a number of difficult and varied courses. She talked about Asian history, literature, calculus, religion, and theater—all courses she was currently taking. As I watched and listened, she communicated in one integrated dialogue, making connections between each of her courses. It was as if all she was learning, and had learned, was integrating before me within the context of her experience. It was mind-blowing to her and for me. As I've watched her evolve through college, she continues to assimilate her education and experience, her self-knowledge (EI), and knowledge of others (RI) in ways that I experience as watching wisdom grow.

Harnessing Our Collective Intelligence (CI)

This book is about Top Teams and what makes them different from other teams. One of the greatest differentiators between adequate teams and Top Teams is in the harnessing and integrating of their members' CI and wisdom accomplished through the process of deliberate and focused dialogue. Think about our lives as educated and smart adults. We take various experiences throughout our lives and continually integrate these discrete but connected events as we develop. Through adulthood and maturity (which tends to be overrated as an experience), we, as learning beings, continue to integrate our experiences—personally, organizationally, and experientially.

Given the amount of information that we are exposed to and bombarded with, we have become intelligent and knowledgeable as individuals. Yet, to the extent that we can develop the requisite EI and RI and then apply them within a global world, we become wiser human beings. Through fully integrating our own knowledge, specialization, and wisdom with that of the people we work with most closely, we create CI—a major differentiator of a Top Team versus a collection of smart and cooperative individuals. This is not something that happens automatically. Rather, it is a constant, deliberate process with incredible payoff.

Matt Ridley (2010), author of *The Rational Optimist: How Prosperity Evolves*, explains that the acceleration of evolution over the past forty-five thousand years—what we refer to as *progress*—is not explainable by evolution alone. Ridley states, "Rather, it is due to collective intelligence: the notion that what determines the inventiveness and the rate of cultural change of a population is the amount of interaction between individuals." He postulates that the "sophistication of the modern world lies not in individual intelligence or imagination, it is a collective enterprise that relies on exchange"—of ideas, thoughts, and commerce.

As Ridley (May 2010) powerfully asserts, *"human takeoff was caused by the invention of the collective brain made possible by the invention of exchange. Once human beings started swapping things and thoughts, they stumbled upon divisions of labor, in which specialization led to mutually beneficial collective knowledge. Specialization is the means by which exchange encourages innovation. In getting better at making your product or delivering your service, you come up with new tools. It is this exchange that makes change collective and cumulative."*

How we mine and utilize the collective IQ of a team *is* the great differentiator between good teams and Top Teams. How we do this is largely dependent on creating a deliberate atmosphere, clear expectations, and agreed-upon processes that can drive the requisite dialogue forward. And this has to occur in a climate that is diverse enough in its experience and specializations that exchange among members produces real value.

Collective Intelligence (CI)—Driving the Process

One of the very common observations we hear from senior leaders about teams that are described as exceptional is that the individual intelligence and experience of the team members is a given. What is different is how people "show up" with one another to utilize this experience and intelligence. We made references to this when we talked about Top Team members' ability to think

> "How we mine and utilize the collective IQ of a team *is* the great differentiator between good teams and Top Teams."

together, to zoom in and zoom out of issues, to be aware of how and how well they dialogue together, and to identity how they process conflict and eventually make decisions.

For the past twenty or so years in working with groups of people and with management teams, we have used a variety of simulations to create opportunities (some familiar and some not) for people to work together and to demonstrate how a team can potentially function better than can a collection of individuals. One of the old standards that is still a favorite of mine is the Subarctic Survival Simulation. This is one of several interesting survival simulations from the firm Human Synergistics. (For more information on Human Synergistics, please see http://www. humansynergistics.com/.)

The premise of the Subarctic Simulation is that a group of people (typically four to seven) on a simulated fishing expedition are involved in a plane crash in a remote area. Their task, first as individuals, then as a team, is to rank-order items they recover from the crash in order of importance to their survival. To do this, they must have a good grasp of the current situation they are in and create a strategy for survival going forward. Sound familiar? When asked to come together as a team and agree on rankings, interesting things happen. Some groups work together well, ensuring that every opinion is heard, that short- and long-term goals are identified, and that decision-making occurs without shutting down communication within the group. The groups that do well generally pay attention to both the rational ordering of items and also to the process by which they operate.

Other groups don't work nearly as well, as the results demonstrate. Certain individuals may dominate, group process is ignored, and occasionally people give up. When

"How do some teams perform far better than the most experienced (a.k.a. smartest) people in the room?"

we debrief the experience by comparing how the groups do against "expert" scores, we almost always see that teams that work together well do better than collections of individuals. These teams often create what is defined as *synergy*—when the collective team has a better result than does the best and most knowledgeable individual on the team. How does this happen? How does a team come together around an unfamiliar situation and make decisions that result in its simulated living or dying together? How do some teams perform far better than the most experienced (a.k.a. smartest) people in the room?

This is a result of mining the CI in such a way that people operate consciously, deliberately, relationally, and logically. Without the right dynamics, most teams fail—some "die" slowly, and others quite quickly. With the right dynamics, most teams survive. Following are two opposite examples.

In the first example, I was debriefing a group made up of engineers, scientists, and managers from a defense contractor. Of the six groups working in the room, one group's members were obviously struggling—but quietly. They were disengaged, heads down, and looked like they'd rather be anywhere else. During the debrief, their individual scores were not bad; in fact, one of the people in this group had a score that resembled that of the experts. Yet this group had come together to "die." What happened? Did they not listen to Fred, who was one of their most knowledgeable members? Did Fred not volunteer his knowledge (he had taught survival training to downed pilots in the military)? I also had the unfamiliar experience of immediately not liking Fred, which is unusual for me. When I asked him about his history and what happened in the group, he said, "They weren't interested in what I had to say, so I shut up." I asked him about his military experience and why he hadn't made a career of it. He said, "They weren't interested in what I had to say ..." This was true of his next two jobs as well. So this was a guy who was smart and experienced, but when faced with disagreement, he disengaged, took his ball and bat, and went home—which resulted in "killing" his team. EI and RI were lacking; thus, the CI could not be brought to bear.

The flip side was a group of women who self-selected themselves as a team within a very macho organization. They interacted with high energy, alternating between intense conversation and laughter. Individually, they had among the lowest scores in the room given the unfamiliarity of the simulation. But together, they were significantly better than any other team. They demonstrated textbook synergy. When I asked them how they performed so well, they said that they understood the rational process of assessing the situation, setting goals, and clarifying how to make decisions. What made the difference for them was their interpersonal and relational process—everyone was engaged. Communication and suggestions were encouraged and supported. They were playful, creative, and serious. They were innovative with ideas. In fact, when they were listing their goals for survival, they created three escalating options:

1. To survive
2. To survive without needing any medical care
3. To survive without needing any medical care and to write a bestseller on wilderness cooking

They blew everybody else away. This was a case of the CI creating a synergy and innovation that beat both all the other groups and the best individuals in the room. Is it unusual? Not really.

If you think about the teams that you are a part of, ask yourself whether the team—and all the people that are there with you—is fully utilizing and integrating the CI and wisdom inherent in the room. If you think of how much knowledge and wisdom each person has integrated and multiply this by the number of people in the room, you have an amazing amount of CI available. The math might even be that being better able to integrate the collective experiences within the room produces an exponential result or step change in CI.

In today's world, people work in teams with great frequency. They initially enter a management team because of a strong track record of performance in a functional or operational area, or they have deep, specialized expertise that a team needs. But despite great platitudes, pictures of rowers on walls, and posters that proclaim, "There is no *I* in team," they tend to struggle when the going gets tough. Developing a team is a conscious and deliberate process. Developing a Top Team, with highly experienced members, is a constant, dialogue-driven, conscious, and deliberate process.

Old Dogs and New Tricks

We have already made the point that for a senior team to become a Top Team, it has to manage the paradox of dealing with the Now and the New. It must manage with an appropriate level of detail orientation, yet be able to handle many complex issues simultaneously. The operating assumption here is that strong teams are well managed, are aligned behind a going-forward strategy, and have a depth of managerial talent and experience to bring to the business.

Why, then, would a successful company mess with an established and successful team? There are several reasons that drive firms to move people in and out of teams, including:

- *Maintaining relevance*: Strong teams often rely on time-tested processes, rhythms, and cadences in their work. The problem is that "we know what we know" attitude. The struggle for mature teams is to maintain relevance in a fast-changing world. Good teams bring with them their own unique and often subtle resistance to change. If it wasn't broke, why break it? Bringing new people in shakes up the system and forces mature teams to rethink their strategy, ways of operating, and how they view the world (and vice versa).

- *Bringing new and diverse thinking to the party*: As we stated in the section on CI, populating the team with ideas and ensuring balance within the paradox of the Now and the New raises the bar of thinking, collective intellect, and challenge. Here's the rub: anecdotal observation and empirical research have concluded that teams that have members with similar makeups form faster, understand one another easier, and operate more smoothly. They also have common blind spots and limitations, which often show up over time. On the other hand, teams that are more diverse (and I use the term broadly to reflect culture, gender, thinking, and personality styles) have a more difficult task in their initial forming and storming. Many never survive that stage. Those that do are more inventive and challenging of one another. They utilize their CI better and, ultimately, have fewer blind spots than the more "vanilla" teams. So the more similar team members are, the greater the challenges are early on. The more diverse the team members are, the better performance is later. It is a conscious choice.

- *Changing demands/changing leaders*: Much of the time, the team that is in a developmental or turnaround stage of an organization functions with very specific and structured goals and with highly directive leadership.

As the organization matures, new people are often brought into the team with different capabilities and an expanded mission. It doesn't always work to rely on, as the adage goes, "who brought you to the dance" as the music changes.

- *Developing leaders*: Many sophisticated organizations with evolved talent management processes deliberately shift high-potential and experienced leaders to different teams to give them a greater variety and depth of experience. Eli Lilly, Johnson Controls, GE, Coca-Cola, and others move people around to give them assignments in different areas or geographies.

Global companies want leaders with global perspectives. They want to ensure that leaders have a comprehensive worldview and experience in dealing with different cultures. However, each and every time the leader moves, the team they are joining must adjust, re-form, build relationships, and mine the diversity that the new person brings (as must the leader who moves).

To the extent that a team is as well developed as the talent management process that staffs it, it will handle the transition intelligently and deliberately. Advances are, perhaps, the best vehicle for orienting a team to its new members, as there is more deliberate narrative of past, present, and future. Building relationships is, of course key to this. Research and practice on executive transitions (as evidenced by Dr. Patricia Wheeler's work on FastForward Transitions) demonstrate that most companies are not fully successful in integrating and accelerating mission-critical people into bigger and broader roles (Wheeler 2010). Defining critical intersections, building a network map, interviewing all "stakeholders," fully understanding the business demands of their new position and the overall business, and creating the essential informal relationships is a deliberate process with great payoff.

But old dogs, even though we love them, must learn new tricks to stay relevant in a world that never stands still. Our job is to provide the process and challenge for them to do so and, whenever possible, turn threat into excitement and opportunity. Curiosity is the antidote to losing relevancy.

Mining for Collective Intelligence (CI) and Social Capital

We live in a time when the intersections of exchange are largely electronic and, as the "millennials" (those born between 1980 and 2000) will tell us, are the ways in which people will connect with one another and do business in the future. While the requirement for face-to-face, highly relational connections within management and senior teams continues to be essential, fostering the environment to expand interaction—creating what is known as social capital—becomes the highway to expanding our network of exchange and, thus, our CI.

In Achieving Success through Social Capital, Wayne Barker (2002) defines social capital as "the resources available in and through personal and business networks." Here he is referencing information, business leads, ideas, opportunities, etc., that can bring diversity to our thinking and experience. While the idea of social networks has been around for some time, the technologies now exist to pull people together in even more powerful ways.

Michel Buffet, a former partner of mine at Mercer-Delta Consulting and now a very smart consultant, has created an approach to assess and deliberately develop social capital within his clients' networks. He begins with "defining the endgame"— what people need from a network going forward. For example, do they need to generate better collaboration and knowledge-sharing across the organization? Do they need to drive innovation and operational speed? Do they need to facilitate faster integration in the context of a merger or acquisition? Or do they need to develop themselves and their team by broadening their network? This is innovative work that is still in its formative stages.

In our FastTime Execution work, our partner, Leland Russell, uses what we call the "Collaboration Center" to bring diverse people and global teams together to populate discussion and grow CI. This utilizes a technology platform to drive dialogue and action learning among and between teams across function and geography. Within smart firms and complex organizations, networks of both like-minded and different people are coming together to—and here is the phrase yet again—*deliberately and consciously* develop their CI within the marketplace of their networks. Very cool stuff.

What Gets in the Way?

There are some obstacles inherent within the CI space:

- *Personal inertia*: Generally, successful people trust what has historically worked for them. Those in the boomer generation, while generally willing to adopt new technologies and ways of operating, have a default setting that may limit willingness to push the boundaries and a tendency to stay with those established networks that have worked for them so far. At worst, this is exemplified by the "good ol' boys network," which is comfortable and successful (until it is not.) Resistance to personal change is also a result of being generally overwhelmed by the amount of "newness" in one's life—technologically, personally, globally, and economically. So while growing a network is understandably the smart thing to do, people of this generation may simply rely on what they know and who they already have in their networks. I do know people who, at this stage in their lives, don't want to meet anybody else. And without a compelling personal and business reason, many will simply "pick their shots" about how, who, and what to engage. Beyond boomers, the millennials have a different sort of resistance to engaging a network to fully mine its CI. I have the pleasure to be around smart and successful "twenty-somethings" who grew up in the information age. Their challenge, as I see it, is one of depth—choosing where to go deep and challenge what they are already thinking. I do not mean to paint this with a broad brush, as I think this is an amazing generation that is evolving. But CI without the requisite EI and RI can read as being smart but not wise. They must work together, and those who have developed their EI and RI are way ahead of the game.

- *System inertia*: There is a tendency to stay with what works unless an organization is either under threat or driven to stay in front. The old line, "The pain of not changing must exceed the pain of change," is applicable. Today, most companies and teams feel either overwhelmed or on the verge of being so. Yet, mining the CI within the organization and within the team is of critical importance. This requires that teams "step back" from day-to-day operations and deliberately think together, solicit new opinions and ways of doing things, define themselves as "learning organizations," and act accordingly.

- *Technical disappointment*: At the time of this writing, LinkedIn is the most popular networking business application. Facebook, Twitter, and others are emerging, but have more of a personal orientation. There are multiple ways of meeting online. But all these are seen as having a half-life as new ways of working evolve. So there is a learning curve to get up to speed, and a concern that getting there isn't going to bring the desired results anyway, as they'll just be something new around the corner.

Emotional Intelligence (EI)/Relational Intelligence (RI)/Collective Intelligence (CI)

In this book, we have talked about the essential need for those on Top Teams to know themselves (EI); to know how to engage, listen, collaborate, deal with conflict, and make decisions (RI); and to ensure that their individual and collective thinking is broadened and deepened by diverse ideas (CI). The notion that we can do any of these without the others is both superficial and suboptimal.

Emotional Intelligence (EI)	Relational Intelligence (RI)	Collective Intelligence (CI)
Knowing oneself	Relating to others	Bringing diverse ideas to the table
Mastering and anticipating emotional states	Listening to and actively engaging others	Intersecting between geographies and functions
Understanding personal default settings and "hot buttons"	Managing the intersections between self, other, and "it"	Creating/ expanding networks
Awareness and respect of differences	Processing differences	Deliberately seeking diversity
Openness/transparency of style	Collaborating	Mining for new thinking
Curiosity about others	Actively seek feedback	Learning to play virtually with others
Deciding and acting on what is important	Making decisions with others	Creating decision rules
Building trust	Building trust	Building trust
Building self-knowledge	Team assessments	Personal networks
Personal/psychological/ personal style assessments	Relevant simulations	Social networking and social network analysis
Individual and 360-degree feedback instruments	Engagement surveys	Technological platforms
EI assessments	Off-site Advances	Culture surveys
	Building informal relationships	Off-site Advances

Top Teams differentiate themselves by utilizing all of the above with an awareness of what they need to do to continue to raise the bar. As Buckminster Fuller used to say, "You can't learn less."

Questions

Harnessing Our Collective Intelligence (CI)

- How well do you utilize the CI of your team? Do you have a deliberate and conscious process to "mine" the CI? Are there things that are present within your team that you rarely get to?

- How diverse is your team (culture, experience, style, ways of thinking, etc.)? Do you take full and complete advantage of that diversity?

- How aware are you, and how aware is your team, of how you dialogue together? Do you deliberately make the effort to utilize the CI present? How do you do that?

- What is possible within this team that you haven't harnessed?

- On a scale of one to ten, how would you rate your experience with CI within your team? Why did you assign this rating? What would it take to be a ten?

Collective Intelligence (CI)—Driving the Process

- In what ways do you utilize CI as a deliberate process within your team?

- Do you utilize simulations or other exercises? If so, what types and what results?

- How do you differentiate between what is good within your team and what is possible?

OLD DOGS AND NEW TRICKS

- How diverse (in the most general definition of the word) is your team?

- What are the advantages of having people who are similar to one another versus having a group that is more diverse and thus more dissimilar?

- Do you have a process to move people in and out of your team?

- How do you transition new people in to guarantee their success?

- How do you deal with the impact of new people on the team?

MINING FOR COLLECTIVE INTELLIGENCE (CI) AND SOCIAL CAPITAL

- How do you utilize the concept and practice of social capital within your work?

- How do you assess and develop your social networks against your developmental needs?

- Do you have a conscious and deliberate process to mine the CI of your team(s)?

WHAT GETS IN THE WAY?

- *Personal inertia*: How do you identify and confront personal inertia/resistance to change and full engagement/utilization with the network?

- *System inertia*: What obstacles does your system or culture create that sub-optimize fully utilizing CI?

- *Technical disappointment*: What processes/software/ programs, etc., work well for you? Where have you been disappointed?

Emotional Intelligence (EI)/Relational Intelligence (RI)/Collective Intelligence (CI)

- How important are EI, RI, and CI to you in your work?

- In what ways are they linked or do they build upon each other?

- In what areas does your team need to improve?

- In what areas can you improve?

- How will you do this?

CHAPTER 10

Being Fully in the Game: Building the Top Team

WE BEGAN THIS BOOK WITH *the story of David, the former general manager of a profitable division of a large manufacturing company. After taking his former division from one that had historically made incremental progress and profit to one that exceeded profit expectations, expanded into adjacent markets, broadened its global footprint, and had grown organically, David was promoted. He left behind a team that knows how to work and think together and has the confidence that it can handle anything that comes its way. He left a division whose engagement scores have gone from average to exceptional. And he left his replacement an organization that deliberately focuses on both the Now and the New, freeing her up to think strategically and optimize her work with that of the larger enterprise. This division is what a good friend refers to as "a happening place."*

In his new position, David again inherited a series of businesses that, for the most part, are strong but uninspired. There is, in his view, a huge gap between "what is" and "what is possible." His challenge as a leader is how to take these businesses to the next level via a process of intense discovery and engagement with the people and teams that report to him. At one level, this goes against his great strength (and potential derailer) of quickly sizing up a business, evaluating its people, and making the immediate decisions necessary to kick-start urgency toward a future he can clearly see. But David learned something in his last position: he learned that the key to achieving these tasks was building Top Teams across and within his businesses or else he would leave no sustainable legacy of change and improvement. So his current challenges can be summarized by the following questions and paradoxes: How does he balance his innate sense of urgency with the need for reasonable patience? How does he get others to see what he sees and operate in ways they've traditionally not known? How does he deliberately and consciously build new Top Teams without them being "David-centric?" How, as a leader, does he balance a hands-on managerial approach with a more "presidential" focus on developing the talent one to three levels down the business?

What Is Versus What Could Be: Seeing the Possibilities

I have what is either a significant character flaw or a great strength. I am unable to look at virtually anything I care about without seeing what might be possible. This is true in my view of the people I love, the restaurants I frequent, the airlines I fly, the work that I do … and the list goes on. Comparing the current reality to what is possible does not always produce a pretty picture unless you can appreciate and acknowledge just how good the current reality is and how the next level could really look. If I cannot acknowledge all that is good with what is, then I often come off as critical. If I cannot understand and honor the history that got it to be as good as it is, then I am at great risk of turning off some of the very people that are tasked with taking it to the next level. Thus it is with teams. On most occasions I am impressed with the caliber of people on the teams that I see—their integrity, commitment, and just how damn hard they work. While I do see my share of "dysfunctional" teams, they represent the exception rather than the rule. More often I see teams that haven't optimized what they are capable of, and in *every* case they know it. They just have rarely been asked.

One of the interview questions I always ask is, "As good as you are, could you raise your level of play?" In every case, across every industry, the answer is "yes." This begs the question, why don't more teams deliberately and consciously move the bar higher? There are several reasons:

1. They are playing flat out as it is and the idea of doing even more seems too much of a stretch.

2. They feel at risk and under threat. They are struggling to make their numbers and keep their promises, so stepping back and working in some different ways gets lost in their urgency.

3. They are doing pretty well and ... well, it's not broke, so why screw around with something good.

But we are talking about Top Teams—teams that have the capabilities to perform at extremely high levels during the toughest of times in the most complex of environments.

> "As good as you are, could you raise your level of play?"

How do Top Teams raise the bar and get even better than they already are?

Making High-Performing Teams into Top Teams

The literature is full of good works about the importance and wisdom of teams, what comprises a good team, and what makes for a dysfunctional one. This book is about how to make good teams even better. It is, at its heart, about creating and sustaining existing and evolving teams into teams that not only survive, but thrive, during tough times. While I am reluctant to create a single "model" for Top Teams, there are some significant differences between solid, high-performing teams and those that operate at the next level.

Much like Herzberg's Two-Factor Theory of Motivation, Top Teams must have a foundation in the many things that define classic high-performing teams. But from there, (Herzberg 1959/1993) Top Teams operate on a different continuum. Another way of describing this is that Top Teams have independent variables that coexist. They require all the very critical behaviors that "high-performance teams" bring, but they operate and elevate with a different and deliberate mindset and process. (See Table 10.1.)

> "How do Top Teams raise the bar and get even better than they already are?"

TABLE 10.1: HIGH-PERFORMANCE TEAMS VS TOP TEAMS

High-Performance Teams	Top Teams
Operate with a compelling vision and a clear-cut mission	Are truly *for* something: they believe in the power of a collective future
Agree on critical business priorities	Embrace and manage the paradox of optimizing both the "Now" and the "New"
Have clearly defined roles, responsibilities, and accountabilities	Work constantly to align the stars: they continually define what the team must be, ensuring the right people are on board and working to build powerful relationships
Identify and resolve issues quickly—process conflict well	Believe in creating trust over peace: everything is on the table in their dialogue with one another
Have well-developed work processes and procedures	Believe in the "Fierce Urgency of the Now," continually improving execution excellence throughout the organization
Have clear behavioral expectations	Believe that dialogue is the basic unit of work and that building trust is essential in working together
Have high individual accountability	Wear an "enterprise hat"; practice individual <u>and</u> collective responsibility for the business
Bring a diversity of skills and experience to the table	Optimize Emotional, Relational, and Collective Intelligence
Operate from a mindset of continuous improvement	Lead change from the front and look for opportunities within a continually shifting external environment

Additionally, *Top Teams* do some things very different than most good teams. They

- Are committed to growing themselves as leaders and as a great Leadership Team
- Operate with passion around what is possible
- Manage complexity yet make the complex understandable
- Regularly step back to look both inward and forward (regular scheduled Advances)
- Demonstrate courage in the face of uncertainty

While I have great respect for "high-performance" teams, they were not designed to drive growth in this complex, "new normal" world that we have talked so much about in this book. In fact, more and more, I see high performance teams as being a "ticket of admission" to becoming a *Top Team*. They provide a solid foundation yet often do not bring the passion, commitment, deliberateness, and courage to operate together in this volatile and fast-changing world.

Throughout this book, I have utilized the terms "deliberate and conscious" to define the difference between a Top Team and a good team. The best leaders from the best organizations I interviewed were thoughtful and deliberate about the continued evolution of their executive team, the leaders on that team, and those people and teams that reported to each of their leaders. As George Bernard Shaw purportedly said, "The worst part of a journey is arriving." In these leaders, there is never any sense of having "arrived." Every person talked about what they could do next, could do even better, and how they might raise the bar. In other words—about what is "possible." This is what makes this work so exciting.

Demonstrating Courage in the Face of Uncertainty: Top Teams in Tough Times

Many years ago, I heard this definition: Courage is an equation composed of doubt plus commitment.

$$Courage = Doubt + Commitment$$

What is it that makes these Top Teams capable of operating in and through tough times? We need little reminder to see how turbulent and unpredictable the world is or how closely we are linked together. Our challenges continue to change, our partnerships broaden, our economies intertwine, our information accelerates, and our politics shift. The paradoxes we are asked to manage only increase in number and complexity. Yet, if we look at how Top Teams operate in tough times, we see important things that do not change: the values and principles, the commitment to success, the determination to leave a legacy, and the sense of how many people rely on them as leaders, friends, and parents. In the face of these waves of change and never-ending responsibilities, how do Top Teams find the courage to get up and face every day with optimism, enthusiasm, and curiosity?

There is no question that doubt, whether it is about how long the economy will fluctuate or whether a firm will retain profitability, is a very real part of the intellectual and emotional fabric of anyone's thinking. Doubt, by itself, is at worst paralytic, and at least distracting. Commitment requires that leadership teams take an active role in crafting a vision of the future and articulating what each individual must expect and do to move forward. US General David Petreaus makes the point that the central role of leaders is to "Get the big ideas right and oversee their implementation by being at the 'point of decision.'" (Petreaus 2010) This is real engagement, where realism and commitment equate to courage. In other words, it is being fully in the game no matter what.

Marshall Goldsmith (2007), in his wonderful book *What Got You Here Won't Get You There,* describes good leaders as operating with a relentless view of the future and embracing those behaviors that reinforce the New. We think of this in our off-site Advances with leadership teams. Unfortunately, many teams are acting as if they are in "retreat" right now, because they believe that their roles and goals are changing or will change with the global economic changes. They are unsure and uncertain about what the criteria for success will be in the years ahead. As mentioned before, an ongoing dialogue process that is connected to the "senior purpose" (what we are *for*) and focused on critical priorities is essential among these executive teams. Introspection and honest review are necessary but insufficient, as any team that aspires to develop has to also look at the future and at what is possible. Then the team has to muster the courage (doubt = commitment) to move toward what is possible. As our friend and good leader Elizabeth Bastoni (personal conversation) suggests, "If you create dialogue in the good times, you have a better chance of having the right conversations when things are going bad."

Jake Jackson (personal conversation), a recently retired senior vice president of a major financial institution, makes the point that leadership teams have a choice: they can go forward with fear or with trust. Jake believes that teams cannot operate successfully and capture opportunities in a tough market if they are governed by fear. Thus, the only choice is to embrace the challenges and go forward with optimism and trust.

Being Fully in the Game

Most of the leaders we interviewed painted a clear picture of creating Top Teams that lead with a mix of reality and optimism, focus on both the Now and the New, and deeply believe in serving others and doing the right thing. One of the most frequent comments we heard was that any decent team can thrive in times of growth or even mediocrity, but only those teams that are "fully in the game" can rise to the occasion and grasp the opportunities when times are tough.

This does not come automatically, even to the best of teams. Operating with conviction, with passion, and with a clear articulation of what the team believes in—what it is *for*—is a conscious and deliberate process. It requires open dialogue. It requires that nothing is hidden and very little is unspoken. It requires an unshakeable belief in the team's ability to have the courage and CI to navigate the future and lead the organization through rough water.

This is what Top Teams do.

Questions

- Think of the team that you are currently on. Are you playing to your full capacity?

- On a scale of one to ten, how good is this team now? Why did you rank it where you did?

- What would it take to be a ten?

- What would you do differently? What would be possible?

- What are some of the obstacles that get in your way?

- Describe those variables that make you a high-performing team. What are those variables that you have to improve upon?

- Look at the variables that describe the behaviors of Top Teams. What do you have to do to make yours a Top Team?

- What does it mean to you to "go forward with trust versus fear?"

- How vocal and/or how well understood are your articulation and passion about your purpose—as individuals and as a team?

APPENDIX

Chapter 1—Setting the Cornerstone: Being Truly FOR Something

BEING TRULY FOR SOMETHING:
THE POWER OF A COLLECTIVE FUTURE

- To what extent is your senior purpose—what you are *for*—clearly understood?

- How well has this been articulated? Does it have passion?

- Can you state it convincingly?

- Does the organization know it? Do individuals know what this means for them and what is expected of them?

WHEN VISION AND REALITY COLLIDE

- How well is the vision of your company understood? Does it represent a desired future for the firm?

- How well do you have your hands around the external realities of your business? Also, how well do you have your hands around your internal realities, capabilities, and limitations?

- Is there a credibility gap between what the senior team has said and what it has done? Are the current realities well articulated and understood by the workforce?

STRATEGY AS PURPOSE

- How "actionable" is your strategic plan? What must the team do to make it even better?

- Are all members clear on how their role drives the plan?

- What is the quality of dialogue within your team? What needs to occur to make it even more open and candid?

INDIVIDUAL AND COLLECTIVE COMMITMENT

- To what extent are you held individually accountable for the success of the team?

- To what extent does the team hold itself collectively accountable?

- What would happen if you raised the bar of collective accountability?

Chapter 2—Aligning the Stars

ONE SIZE DOES NOT FIT ALL:
WHAT KIND OF TEAM DO WE NEED TO BE?

- Given the mission and purpose of the organization (what we are *for*), what kind of team do we need to be to accomplish these?

- What are our critical priorities and accountabilities?

- Do we have the right people on the bus?

- How should we be structured to optimize decisions?

- Where are our critical interdependencies? How do we best reach across functions and geographies?

- How do we work together to lead the organization in these times?

- What does it mean to be a leader in this company today?

DEFINING AND MANAGING THE CRITICAL INTERSECTIONS

- How do I best navigate the matrix and work across the enterprise?

- Have I created a system map that defines my critical intersections?

- Have I "made and cut my deals" with the people with whom I have critical interdependencies?

- Am I able, and willing, to be direct and honest with these people to ensure that all issues are on the table?

TRUST OVER PEACE:
ADDRESSING AND RESOLVING THE ISSUES THAT MATTER

- How direct am I (are we) with one another?

- To what extent do indirect, third-party conversations occur?

- How well have we "institutionalized conflict"? How willing are we to surface tough issues and talk them through?

- What issues, historical or current, get in the way of our ability to trust one another?

- Who do I have to build a better relationship with? When and how?

SHAVING THE TIGER:
UNDERSTANDING AND RECALIBRATING
THE DEFAULT SETTING OF A TEAM

- How would I describe the "default setting" of our team when under pressure?

- What assessments or instruments have we used that have provided information on our individual and collective default settings?

- How well have we articulated the "rules of the road" and what to do to sustain real teamwork?

- How would I describe my personal default setting when under stress?

- How have we built a collective EI?

- How well do we know ourselves?

- How do you measure the progress of your team?

- What objective markers do you utilize to define progress?

- What are the subjective experiences that allow you to know, with a high degree of certainty, that you are moving forward as a team?

- What is your level of enthusiasm and optimism in moving forward with your team?

Chapter 3—Focusing on the Now and the New

THE NOW AND THE NEW

- Describe several of the paradoxes you are facing as a management team.

- In your dialogue together, how are these handled? Are they identified as paradoxes to be managed or problems to be solved?

- What are the top two paradoxes that must be fully discussed? What value might come from this discussion?

- What venues/opportunities do you have as a leadership team to discuss the "big" issues?

- Are you fully harnessing the CI of your team?

ENCOURAGING AND NORMALIZING PARADOX

- What are the three to five key paradoxes your team faces?

- How well do you, as a team, identify and discuss important issues that are paradoxes?

- If time is a valuable commodity for you and your team, when do you find the opportunities to discuss the big issues?

Driving the Fierce Urgency of "Now": The Need for Execution Excellence

- How would you rate the quality of your execution against your strategic plan? What has happened so far? What must change to make this even more effective?

- What does the concept of "speed" mean in your business and to you personally? Can you and should you accelerate it?

- What obstacles are in the way of executing—with speed—in your company?

- How well has your team/leadership articulated the compelling business reasons behind the changes throughout your company? What has been the result?

- How is the workforce engaged in this process? How could this be improved?

Allowing Optionality and Possibility

- How well do you, as a leadership team, value and harness your CI?

- What would it take to raise the bar? What would be the value?

- How safe is it to challenge fundamental business assumptions? How safe is it to talk about optionality within your team?

- Is the fundamental backdrop of trust present within your team to challenge your performance against the Now and the New?

Chapter 4—Wrap Your Head around Change

Has Change ... Changed?

- How has the nature of change ... changed for you?

- What have been some of the most significant changes to impact your business in the past three years?

- What have been some of the most disruptive changes to you in that time?

- Describe where you see increased VUCA (volatility, uncertainty, complexity, and ambiguity) in your world and within your organization?

- What has been the impact on you and on other leaders?

- How well is your team talking about and handling the changes that you describe?

- What could you do even better?

Models of Change: What Works in the New Normal?

- How thoroughly have you and your team talked about those changes that impact you?

- How well do you understand the dynamics and potential impact of change on your team and on the workforce?

- Do you have a model of change that you follow?

- Do you deliberately try to predict what may occur and prepare alternatives?

- How able and agile is your company in responding to unexpected changes?

Optimizing Control and Predictability: Taking Care of You and Them

- How proactive are you with your workforce in discussing potential and possible disruptive change? Do you normalize it?

- How involved and engaged are they in crafting responses to changes?

- Do you remind them about what is *not* changing in the company?

- Do you actively coach your players about how best to respond to VUCA?

Be Visible and Talk Straight

- What are you doing to ensure clear communication with the workforce?

- How do you know how they are responding and their view of leadership?

- Where could you be even more proactive and communicative?

- In what ways have you utilized these complex and uncertain times to build opportunities for your business? How have you used the "burning platform" for change?

- How have you grown as a leader?

Chapter 5—Essential Navigational Skills

Making the Complex Understandable

- How crisp and clear is your going-forward strategy?

- Is it clearly understood by all members of your senior team?

- How well is it understood by the workforce? Do they get both the expectations of the Now and the strategy for the New?

- How well can people link their roles to the critical priorities for the organization?

Deciding How to Decide

- How quickly and accurately do you make decisions within your team?

- Do you have an agreed-upon decision-making model in place?

- On a scale of one to ten, rate the quality and speed of your decision process. What would it take to be a ten?

- Do you "label" how each decision will be made?

Navigating the Formal and Informal Organizations

- How do you define the "formal organization" in your company?

- How does it work? What are the spoken and unspoken rules?

- How in touch are you with the "informal organization?" How do you know?

- In what way does the informal organization "push back"? Who are the key influencers within the informal organization?

Engagement: Waxing the Forklift

- How do you measure the engagement of your workforce against your critical priorities?

- How well do what the formal organization says and what the informal organization does match up?

- Do you have behavioral ground rules that people understand and follow?

Responsibility: The Real Story

- What is your definition of "responsibility"?

- What is the limitation of believing that you and another each have 50 percent of the responsibility for an outcome?

- Think of a situation that you approach as if you are 100 percent responsible for the outcome, and everything and everybody else is 0 percent responsible. What changes as a result? How difficult is it?

Chapter 6—The Art of the Advance: How Good Teams Get Even Better

THE NEED FOR HIGH-ORDER DIALOGUE

- Who is the dominant force behind your culture? What kind of culture does this create?

- What are the behaviors in your organization that lead to public agreement but private complaining? What is the cost to the organization?

- To what extent do people on your team feel able to shoot straight, differ publicly, raise different ideas, and dialogue fully?

- Do you rate the quality of your meetings? Do you occasionally stop in the middle of a meeting and ask how it can be improved? What would be the value in doing so?

- In your team, how candid are you with one another? Do you leave meetings with unaddressed and unresolved issues? What is the cost of doing so?

- What do you do to deliberately improve your ability as a team to truly engage issues and create effective dialogue?

- Does your CEO/leader trust you to tell the full truth?

DIFFERENTIATING AN ADVANCE FROM A RETREAT

- How often does your team have an Advance—a meeting designed to produce open and real dialogue about the most important issues?

- How often do you revisit your strategy and assess what is changing in your world?

- How often do you adjust your priorities?

- Can you, and do you, talk as a team about the issues that get in your way? Think about one or two issues that are unspoken but important to talk about. What would it take to do this inside your team? What would you gain if you did this well?

- How open, how candid, and how productive are you in your dialogue together? What could make this even better?

- Do you regularly do after action reviews (AARs)? How would you make the next meeting even better than this one?

Interview as Intervention

- How often do you have an experienced third party interview members of the team to assure that the important issues are making it to the table?

- Who is around that knows the team, the players, the business, the dynamics, the default settings, and how the team could be even better?

Dynamics, Dynamics, Dynamics

- How would you describe the dynamics within your team? What are the positive dynamics that make you as good as you are? What are the underlying dynamics that interfere with your being a Top Team?

- Do you have a process for surfacing and addressing the dynamics inherent within your team?

- Do the unsaid things get said? Are there "unmentionables" around which people tread lightly?

- How would it improve your team performance if you were "clean"—in other words, if nothing important was left unsaid?

CALLING AUDIBLES

- Are your off-sites driven by and wedded to very specific agendas?

- How flexible are you, as a team, in calling audibles that change your direction when necessary?

- Can you give an example in which calling an audible changed your direction in a very positive and productive way?

CREATING RULES OF ENGAGEMENT

- Do you have well-articulated behavioral agreements between team members?

- Do they apply back at the office?

- Are these agreements understood and utilized across the larger organization?

- Is this how the informal organization operates?

Chapter 7—Growing and Sustaining Top Teams

BUILDING RELATIONAL INTELLIGENCE (RI)

- How have you used Emotional Intelligence (EI) to build increased self-awareness as a leader?

- How have you used data from 360s, style assessments, conflict inventories, etc., to develop your leadership effectiveness?

- Has this been sustainable? Does it retain value over time for you?

- How would you define RI?

Relational Intelligence (RI) and Top Teams

- How deliberate and conscious are you and members of your team in creating RI to improve collaboration, ideation, and trust within your team?

- To what extent do you spend time together informally to build RI and get to know one another?

Relational Capital and Trust

- How willing are you to "say the next thing," to challenge your peers, to ask for support, to trust their intention toward you?

- How do you link RI, trust, collaboration, and effectiveness together?

- What would increased trust look like in your team?

- How deliberate is your practice of building RI within your team and across your network?

It's Always about Communication

- How well do members of your team communicate— really communicate—with one another?

- Do people on your team know what you are really *for*? Do you know what they are *for*?

- Do you understand the obstacles they have to achieving their purpose? Do others know your obstacles?

- What would it be like if communication were even better than it is?

Zooming in and Zooming out

- How well does your team zoom in (get into the details, numbers, and tactics)?

- How well does it zoom out (see the larger picture, context, and systemic view)?

- What is the default setting of the team?

- Do you have the capabilities to do both well?

- What could you do even better? What would be the payoff?

Collaborate to Calibrate:
Building Teams One to Three Levels Down

- How well do you talk about talent against the leadership needs of the company?

- Do you look at high performers' EI, RI, and CI in addition to their track records of performance?

- How well do executives "coach" their subordinates, high potentials, and one another in the service of building the team(s) and achieving the strategy?

- How deliberate are you in engaging and building teams one to three levels below you?

- How could you and your organization be better leadership developers, coaches, and mentors? What is the payoff?

Chapter 8—Being "That" Person: Great Teams Need Great Leaders

The Person of the Leader:
Being Conscious and Deliberate

- How diverse is your team in terms of style, experience, and ways of thinking?

- To what extent are you, as a team, committed to continuing your individual and collective development as leaders and as a team?

- How do you ensure this occurs, given your time constraints?

- How often do you schedule "special time" off-site to explore issues, confirm your operating assumptions, and improve your level of play together?

- How often do you spend time rehearsing scenarios and deliberately thinking together?

- When was the last time you thought about how you think together?

- How often and how thoroughly do you do after action reviews (AARs)?

- Are these debriefs, postmortems, or explorations into what you learned and what you might do differently?

- Do you directly and frequently ask your teammates the question, "How can I help you?"

Coaching in Context

- How does your company utilize coaching?

- In your opinion, how well does it work?

- What has been your experience?

- What could your company do to improve the process to make it even better?

Experience Matters—Ten Thousand Hours

- Do you believe that the deep experience of a coach (ten thousand hours) really matters?

- How do you assess a coach's experience and background?

- How important is it for a coach to have a strong background in understanding personality style and interpersonal dynamics?

- Does a coach need to have an understanding of the business and the system that a person works within to be fully effective?

It's Lonely at the Top

- Who do you talk to?

- Can you discuss virtually anything ("put the moose on the table") with your team?

- Do you have a close-in and trusted advisor who knows your team and your business?

"You Can't Learn Less"—Leadership Development that Works

- How sustainable and lasting has your experience with leadership training been?

- What experiences have been most valuable for you personally and for your team?

- In terms of leadership development and training, what works and what doesn't?

Sustainability: The Human Side

- Do you generally know what is going on with other members of your team? Do you express interest and genuinely care about how they are doing?

- Do you talk to one another about the pressures of the job?

Chapter 9—The Power of Integration

Harnessing Our Collective Intelligence (CI)

- How well do you utilize the CI of your team? Do you have a deliberate and conscious process to "mine" the CI? Are there things that are present within your team that you rarely get to?

- How diverse is your team (culture, experience, style, ways of thinking, etc.)? Do you take full and complete advantage of that diversity?

- How aware are you, and how aware is your team, of how you dialogue together? Do you deliberately make the effort to utilize the CI present? How do you do that?

- What is possible within this team that you haven't harnessed?

- On a scale of one to ten, how would you rate your experience with CI within your team? Why did you assign this rating? What would it take to be a ten?

Collective Intelligence (CI)—Driving the Process

- In what ways do you utilize CI as a deliberate process within your team?

- Do you utilize simulations or other exercises? If so, what types and what results?

- How do you differentiate between what is good within your team and what is possible?

Old Dogs and New Tricks

- How diverse (in the most general definition of the word) is your team?

- What are the advantages of having people who are similar to one another versus having a group that is more diverse and thus more dissimilar?

- Do you have a process to move people in and out of your team?

- How do you transition new people in to guarantee their success?

- How do you deal with the impact of new people on the team?

Mining for Collective Intelligence (CI) and Social Capital

- How do you utilize the concept and practice of social capital within your work?

- How do you assess and develop your social networks against your developmental needs?

- Do you have a conscious and deliberate process to mine the CI of your team(s)?

- *Personal inertia*: How do you identify and confront personal inertia/resistance to change and full engagement/utilization with the network?

- *System inertia*: What obstacles does your system or culture create that sub-optimize fully utilizing CI?

- *Technical disappointment*: What processes/software/ programs, etc., work well for you? Where have you been disappointed?

Emotional Intelligence (EI)/ Relational Intelligence (RI)/Collective Intelligence (CI)

- How important are EI, RI, and CI to you in your work?

- In what ways are they linked or do they build upon each other?

- In what areas does your team need to improve?

- In what areas can you improve?

- How will you do this?

Chapter 10—Being Fully in the Game: Building the Top Team

Think of the team that you are currently on. Are you playing to your full capacity?

- On a scale of one to ten, how good is this team now? Why did you rank it where you did?

- What would it take to be a ten?

- What would you do differently? What would be possible?

- What are some of the obstacles that get in your way?

- Describe those variables that make you a high-performing team. What are those variables that you have to improve upon?

- Look at the variables that describe the behaviors of Top Teams. What do you have to do to make yours a Top Team?

- What does it mean to you to "go forward with trust versus fear?"

- How vocal and/or how well understood are your articulation and passion about your purpose—as individuals and as a team?

BIBLIOGRAPHY

Appel, Boyce. Personal conversation with the author. Permission to use granted.

Barker, Wayne. *Achieving Success though Social Capital: Tapping the Hidden Resources in Your Personal and Business Networks.* New York: Jossey-Bass, 2002.

Bastoni, Elizabeth. Personal conversation with the author. Permission to use granted.

Campbell, Robert MD. Personal conversation with the author. Permission to use granted.

Charan, Ram. "Conquering a Culture of Indecision," *Harvard Business Review OnPoint Enhanced Edition*, April 2001: 1–11.

Collins, Jim. *Good to Great: Why Some Companies Make the Leap ... and Others Don't.* New York: HarperCollins, 2001.

Conference Board: *CEO Confidence Survey*, 2007.

Connolly, Mickey, and Richard Rianoshek. *The Communication Catalyst.* Chicago, IL: Dearborn Trade Publishing, 2002: 145.

Connolly, Mickey. Personal conversation with the author. Permission to use granted.

Darrow, Clarence. As quoted in "Improving the Quality of Life for the Black Elderly: Challenges and Opportunities : Hearing before the Select Committee on Aging, House of Representatives, One Hundredth Congress, first session, September 25, 1987 (1988)."

DeBono, Edward. *De Bono's Thinking Course.* New York: Facts on File, 1982.

Finan, Irial. Personal conversation with the author. Permission to use granted.

Fuller, R. Buckminster. *Critical Path.* New York: St. Martin's Press, 1981.

Gladwell, Malcolm. *Outliers: The Story of* Success. New York: Little, Brown, & Co., 2008.

Goldsmith, Marshall. http://www.marshallgoldsmithlibrary.com/. Accessed 03-02-11.

Goldsmith, Marshall. *What Got You Here Won't Get You There: How Successful People Become Even More Successful.* New York: Hyperion, 2007.

Herzberg, Frederick, Bernard Mausner, and Barbara Block Snyderman. *The Motivation to Work.* New York: John Wiley & Sons, 1959. Revised edition: New Brunswick, NJ: Transaction Publishers, 1993.

Hrebiniak, Lawrence. "Working Council for Chief Financial Officers, Balanced Scorecard." Collaborative Bain & Co., *strategy+business.* http://en.wikipedia.org/wiki/Volatility,_uncertainty,_complexity_and_ambiguity. Accessed 03/03/11.

Jackson, Jake. Personal conversation with the author. Permission to use granted.

Johnson, Barry. *Polarity Management: Identifying and Managing Unsolvable Problems.* Amherst, MA: HRD Press, 1992/1996.

Kesseler, Brian. Personal conversation with the author. Permission to use granted.

Kim, W. Chan, and Renee Mauborgne. *Blue Ocean Strategy: How to Create Uncontested Market Space and Make Competition Irrelevant.* Boston, MA: Harvard Business School Publishing, 2005.

Koestenbaum, Peter. *Leadership: The Inner Side of Greatness.* New York: Jossey-Bass, 1991: 33.

Kotter, John P. *Leading Change.* Boston, MA: Harvard Business School Press, 1996.

Lencioni, Patrick. *Death by Meeting: A Leadership Fable ... About Solving the Most Painful Problem in Business.* New York: Jossey-Bass, 2004.

Lencioni, Patrick. *The Five Dysfunctions of a Team: A Leadership Fable.* New York: Jossey-Bass, 2002.

Levin, Lawrence, and Leland A. Russell. "High Velocity Execution," *Leading News Teleforum*, September 25, 2008.

MacKinnon, Bill. Personal conversation with the author. Permission to use granted.

Melville, Iain. Personal conversation with the author. Permission to use granted.

Myers, Dave. Personal conversation with the author. Permission to use granted.

Nadler, David A. *Champions of Change: How CEOs and Their*

Companies Are Mastering the Skills of Radical Change. New York: Jossey-Bass, 1998.

Petreaus, David. "Military and Pentagon Leaders Urge Patience for Afghan Mission" www.nytimes.com/2010/06/17/world/17military.html/. Accessed 03-02-11.

Ridley, Matt. "Humans: Why They Triumphed," *Wall Street Journal,* May 22, 2010.

Ridley, Matt. *The Rational Optimist: How Prosperity Evolves.* New York: Harper, 2010.

Wall, Nick. Personal conversation with the author. Permission to use granted.

Warden III, John A., and Leland A. Russell. *Winning in Fast Time: Harness the Competitive Advantage of Prometheus in Business and Life.* Los Angeles, CA, GEO Group Press, 2001.

Wheeler, Patricia. "Making Successful Transitions: The Leader's Perspective." *The AMA Handbook of Leadership,* eds. Marshall Goldsmith, John Baldoni, and Sarah McArthur. New York: AMACOM, 2010): 187.

Wheeler, Patricia. Personal conversation with the author. Permission to use granted.

Wolfgang von Goethe, Johann. http://www.quotedb.com/quotes/2784. Accessed 03-02-11.

About the Author

Over the past eighteen years I have helped senior teams from many different industries learn to navigate growth, manage significant and complex change, and address the new and ever-changing global marketplace and economies. These are smart people doing what is "business as usual" for a top team—or at least should be. Top Teaming is the culmination of the knowledge and experiences I have had in working intimately with top teams—and those striving to improve their effectiveness. It describes what is necessary to make a good team, even a high-performing team, even better.

Working with Senior Teams is not only a profession—it is a passion and a privilege. These are incredibly talented, committed, and hard-working people who create something very special when they move beyond the classic, expected "high-performing team" to a real Top Team. To see real collaboration and collective intelligence in action is both exciting and inspiring.

I live in Atlanta, Georgia, with my wife and business partner, Dr. Patricia Wheeler—one of the finest executive coaches working today. I have two wonderful daughters, a big assortment of unusual friends, and am blessed (or cursed) with insatiable curiosity.

To learn even more about how to apply the Top Teaming principles and to access the Top Teaming Assessment, please visit my website at www.TheLevinGroup.com .

To make the *Top Teaming* process a reality in your company, please visit our website at www.TheLevinGroup.com to review:

- ✓ **Additional Information about our Services**
- ✓ **Connection to our newsletter, blogs and teleforums**
- ✓ **A Sample Top Teaming Assessment™**

Top Teaming Assessment™:
The Top Teaming Assessment is the first significant step in moving a team from a group of very competent and hard-working leaders into a Top Team. This on-line assessment provides a very clear picture of how a team is currently operating against where <u>they</u> say they need to be functioning.

We use this assessment as the basis of a full day "advance" in which your team addresses the questions above and gets clarity on:

- What kind of team are you? What kind of team do you need to be? What are the gaps?
- How to drive critical priorities in your organization
- Defining and navigating critical intersections between roles
- Creating trust, candor, and openness within your team
- Creating an "energy audit" to get the most important things done
- Driving execution and operational excellence
- Developing your leaders and teams 1-3 levels down

The outcome of the day is agreement on driving the critical few priorities needed for your team to "raise their game," clarity about how to do this, and the value in doing so.

Please visit our website at www.TheLevinGroup.com for a sample assessment

To order this book:
For Information about ordering the book *Top Teaming: A Roadmap for Leadership Teams Navigating the Now, the New, and the Next*, please see our website at
www.TopTeaming.com